The CONCEPT of GOD

Ronald H. Nash

Academie Books Grand Rapids, Michigan
Zondervan Publishing House

ACADEMIE BOOKS are published by Zondervan Publishing House,
1415 Lake Drive, S.E., Grand Rapids, Michigan 49506

THE CONCEPT OF GOD
Copyright © 1983 by The Zondervan Corporation
Grand Rapids, Michigan

Library of Congress Cataloging in Publication Data
Nash, Ronald H.
  The concept of God.

  Bibliography: p.
  Includes index.
    1. God—Attributes.   2. Theism.   I. Title.
BT130.N37   1983   231'.4   83-6757
ISBN 0-310-45141-8

Edited by Jack Stewart
Designed by Louise Bauer

Printed in the United States of America

        86 87 88 — 10 9 8 7 6 5 4 3

To
Neva Perry
and
to the memory of
Florence T. Perry

Contents

◆

Preface

◆

    This book is an invitation to think about God. It is an exploration in philosophical theology that focuses on classical and contemporary discussions of the divine attributes, especially as difficulties with those attributes are believed to raise doubts about the coherence of the concept of God. The days when philosophers were content just to ask if God exists are gone forever. Of course, they will continue to discuss the traditional arguments for God's existence. But in recent years, the attention of philosophers has been directed to an entirely different and more fundamental set of issues. The question today is not "Does God exist?" but "Is it logically possible for God to exist?" Many philosophers believe it is possible to show that the concept of God found in theistic religions such as Christianity, Judaism, and Islam is the picture of a logically impossible being.

    I have limited my discussions to Christian theism. But because the Christian concept of God shares most of its essential claims about God with Judaism and Islam, the observations of this book will be relevant to those faiths as well. Representatives of Judaism and Islam in the Middle Ages contributed much to the development of the views that we shall consider.

    Most of the material on which this book draws appears in books and professional journals that are often inaccessible and, I regret to add, unintelligible to the general reader. Almost all of these publications have been addressed to professional philosophers and thus presuppose a familiarity with technical issues in logic, metaphysics, epistemology, and the philosophy of language. Because I believe it is valuable to make the content of those more technical discussions available to a wider audience, I have tried to write this book at an introductory level. Those who use this work as their introduction to the literature will find it easier

9

to work through the more technical discussions which are cited in the notes and bibliography.

These reflections about God will probably not inspire much in the way of reverence or personal piety. Any reader seeking that kind of inspiration should look elsewhere. I do think, however, that the kind of inquiry conducted in this book can be a helpful propaedeutic for the more practical dimensions of religion.

Dr. Larry Mayhew, my colleague at Western Kentucky University, deserves a special word of thanks for the many helpful comments he offered during the writing of the manuscript. Jack Stewart did a first-rate editorial job. Help also came from other colleagues including Ted Schoen, Robert Roberts, Arvin Vos, and James Spiceland.

Chapter 1

Some Preliminary Considerations

Philosophical reflection about God has taken a new turn. During the past fifteen or twenty years, American and British philosophers have written a surprisingly large number of books and articles on various issues related to the concept of God. These philosophical investigations usually focus on one or two of the divine attributes and normally include some analysis of what the attributes mean. In many of these writings, traditional Christian theism comes under attack from one of two different directions: (1) Some allege that theism is internally inconsistent, from which it follows that the God of theism is a logically impossible being. This constitutes a new and powerful argument for atheism. (2) Another group of thinkers rejects the atheist's conclusions and argues instead that the classical concept of God must be modified in several dramatic ways. This second procedure is adopted by advocates of the increasingly influential school of Process theology. According to the first challenge, Christian theism must be *abandoned* because its concept of God is incoherent. According to the second, the classical Christian concept of God must be *replaced* by the substitute offered by Process theology.

I intend to show that the conclusions of the atheist and the process theologian are premature. A theistic concept of God is still viable, even though a major rethinking of several aspects of its package of attributes may be required.

THE CONCEPT OF GOD

A concept of God may be thought of as a cluster or package of properties attributed to the divine being. The phrase *package of attributes* suggests that the properties attributed to God are tied together in some way. I can go still further, and speak of the set of divine attributes as a *logical* package, which is simply a way of saying they must fit together logically; the entire cluster of divine attributes must be logically consistent. Any concept of God that contained logically incompatible attributes would picture a logically impossible being. Whatever else may be true about a logically impossible being, it cannot exist. With respect to any proposed concept of God, then, it is proper to ask if the various elements of the concept fit together, if they are logically consistent. The concept of God found in Christian theism must pass the test of logical consistency.

In recent debate, the question of the consistency or coherence of the concept of God has taken four different forms:

1. Each individual attribute must be self-consistent. Some philosophers have maintained, for example, that the very concept of an omnipotent being is logically incoherent. Sometimes this assertion has been based upon certain paradoxes said to be generated by the notion of omnipotence. One such paradox begins by asking whether an omnipotent being can create a stone too heavy for it to lift. If the question is answered affirmatively, then supposedly there is one thing an omnipotent being cannot do; he cannot lift the stone that is too heavy to lift. On the other hand, if the question is answered negatively, there is something else an omnipotent being cannot do; he cannot create the stone in question. In either case, an "omnipotent" being faces a task he cannot perform. Because the concept of an omnipotent being generates such a paradox, it is dismissed as incoherent. Similar challenges have been raised about the coherence of other divine attributes such as omniscience, timelessness, simplicity, and necessity. All of these properties have been alleged to be self-contradictory. Anyone who wishes to preserve the intellectual integrity of theism must answer such charges.

2. Divine attributes must be logically compatible with each other. Some thinkers have claimed that two or more divine attributes are logically incompatible. Anthony Kenny has written that "the traditional doctrines of omniscience and omnipotence cannot be stated in a way which makes them compatible with other traditional doctrines such as that of divine immutability."[1] According to one argument used to show that God's omniscience is incompatible with his immutability, God must know everything, including what time it is. But time changes. Therefore, if God is omniscient and knows everything, He knows some things that change which entails that He changes. Thus, God cannot be immutable.* It is sometimes asserted that an incoherence exists between the attributes of omnipotence and timelessness. How can a timeless being (a being completely removed from time) be Creator of a

---

[1] Anthony Kenny, *The God of the Philosophers* (Oxford: Clarendon Press, 1979), p. 10.

*The fallacies in this argument will be discussed in a later chapter.

temporal world? Supposedly, the Creation took place at a particular time. But how can a being be timeless and yet create a temporal world, an event that had a location in time? Moreover, how can a timeless God sustain a world of temporal processes?

3. Divine attributes must be consistent with other important concerns within a particular theological system. Kenny, whose doubts about the compatibility of omniscience and immutability have already been noted, wonders, for example, if the divine attributes of omnipotence and omniscience are consistent with such central Christian convictions as God's "lack of responsibility for sin, and human freedom of the will."[2] Most Christian theists have believed it is important to preserve some kind of human freedom. But how can human free choice be affirmed in conjunction with the belief that an omniscient God has total and perfect knowledge about the future? If God knows everything that is going to happen in the future, how can any future event occur other than in accord with the divine foreknowledge? Does not God's foreknowledge make the future necessary?

4. Finally and most important, for theism to be coherent demands that the concept of God itself be consistent, not contradictory. David Blumenfeld boldly announces that "the concept of God is contradictory."[3] Blumenfeld makes it clear that the target of his attack is "the standard Judeo-Christian theological conception of divinity, a being who is by definition absolutely perfect."[4] Such a challenge dare not be taken lightly by the theist. After all, as Kenny explains:

> Anyone who is interested in the question of the existence of God has to study first of all the divine attributes; for to say that God exists is to say that there is something that has the divine attributes; and if "God exists" is to be true, then the divine attributes must at least themselves be coherent and jointly compatible. The coherence of the notion of God, as possessor of the traditional attributes, is a necessary, though of course not sufficient, condition for God's existence.[5]

If a particular concept of God is logically contradictory, then it is logically impossible for such a God to exist. The incoherence of the concept of God would provide an inescapable argument against the existence of such a God.

Logical coherence and the concept of God are related in one additional way. Richard Swinburne asks, "Are there any logical relations between the predicates ascribing properties to God or are they just

---

[2]Kenny, *The God of the Philosophers*, p. 11.

[3]David Blumenfeld, "On the Compossibility of the Divine Attributes," *Philosophical Studies* 34 (1978): 91.

[4]Ibid.

[5]Kenny, *The God of the Philosophers*, p. 5.

a string of predicates, such that it is coherent to suppose that there might be beings with different combinations of them?" Adopting the first view, Swinburne illustrates his point by suggesting it is logically necessary that an omniscient and perfect free deity "be perfectly good, and that a perfectly good creator of the universe . . . be a source of moral obligation."[6] He also argues that a being who is both omnipotent and omniscient must of necessity be an omnipresent spirit.

> A person who is omnipotent is able to bring about effects everywhere by basic actions. One who is omniscient at a certain time has justified true beliefs about all things which are going on anywhere at that time. . . . An omniscient being does not depend for his knowledge on the correct functioning of intermediaries. Hence an omnipotent and omniscient person, in my senses of the terms, is of logical necessity an omnipresent spirit.[7]

In many instances, a particular divine attribute will logically entail certain other attributes. For example, theists often maintain that the attribute of timelessness entails the attribute of immutability. If God is timeless, then He must also be immutable. The very possibility of change presupposes a "before" and "after." If a being is such that no "before" or "after" is possible with respect to its being (and this is certainly true of a timeless being), then it is logically impossible for that being to change. But immutability also entails timelessness. If God is incapable of change in any way, then God must be timeless.[8] Whether or not all of the given examples turn out to be correct, it does seem clear that logical entailments between different attributes have the effect of producing different packages of attributes and thus different concepts of God.

THE FUNCTION OF THE WORD GOD

One thing that must be settled early in my discussion is how the word God functions in traditional discourse. More specifically, is the word God a proper name? One reason this question has been thought important is the existence of a rather influential tradition stemming from the nineteenth-century British philosopher, John Stuart Mill. Advocates of Mill's position hold that proper names do not function as descriptive expressions. While proper names denote or refer to specific individuals, they do not connote any collection of properties. In short, proper names have no meaning. If this view is correct (and there are

---

[6]Richard Swinburne, *The Coherence of Theism* (Oxford: Clarendon Press, 1977), p. 222.

[7]Ibid., pp. 222, 223.

[8]For an elaboration of this claim, see Nelson Pike, *God and Timelessness* (New York: Schocken, 1970), pp. 39ff.

many who think it is not) and if the word *God* functions as a proper name, then such important traditional statements such as "God is good" could conceivably be false. But many theists have wanted to maintain that a statement like "God is good" does not just happen to be true; it is necessarily true in the sense that denying it would be as self-contradictory as affirming that a circle is square.

In an attempt to preserve this intuition, Nelson Pike argues that "God" is *not* a proper name. Instead, Pike maintains, "God" functions as a special kind of descriptive expression that he calls a *title*. As Pike explains, "Grammatically, title-phrases are descriptive expressions that often do the work of proper names and that often appear in linguistic environments similar to those associated with proper names."[9] An example of what Pike has in mind is the title *Caesar*, which was used both as a name and as a descriptive expression. As its usage evolved, "Caesar" became more than a proper name; it came to be applied legitimately only to persons who occupied a particular position.

> A title is a term used to mark a certain position or value-status as does, e.g., "Caesar" in the sentence "Hadrian is Caesar." To say that Hadrian is Caesar is to say that Hadrian occupies a certain governmental position; more specifically, it is to say that Hadrian is Emperor of Rome. To affirm of some individual that He is God is to affirm that that individual occupies some special position (e.g., that He is Ruler of the Universe) or that that individual has some special value-status (e.g., that He is a being greater than which cannot be conceived).[10]

Pike seems to be on the right track. In the Christian tradition, the word *God* is not a proper name that can be rightfully applied to any Tom, Dick, or Harry. As Christians use the word, *God* is a descriptive term. Its meaning includes such notions as ruler of the universe, Creator of the universe, and the perfect being. As a title having descriptive significance, *God* should only be given to a properly qualified being. As Pike continues, "It is a logically necessary condition of bearing the title 'God' . . . that the individual bearing the title be perfectly good, omnipotent, omniscient and the like."[11] Once the word *God* is understood in this way, it can only be applied to the kind of being who serves as a particular instance of the properties connoted by the title. Sentences like "God is perfectly good," "God is omnipotent," and "God is omniscient" turn out to be necessary truths. The denial of any such statement is a logical contradiction.

---

[9]Ibid., p. 29.
[10]Nelson Pike, "Omnipotence and God's Ability to Sin," *American Philosophical Quarterly* 6 (1969): 208.
[11]Pike, *God and Timelessness*, p. 33.

ESSENCE AND ATTRIBUTE

A divine attribute is an essential property of God. A property is essential to some being if and only if the loss of that property entails that that being ceases to exist. A divine attribute is a property which God could not lose and continue to be God.

The distinction between essential and nonessential properties first appears clearly in the writings of Aristotle. Aristotle pointed out that many properties of a thing are nonessential (or accidental) in the sense that they could be changed without affecting the essence of the thing. A table, for example, could be painted a different color or moved to a different location or made shorter or taller; but it would still be a table. Its essence would be unchanged. All changes like the examples cited would affect only nonessential characteristics of the table. But it would also be possible to change the table in ways that would alter it so drastically that it would no longer be a table. One might, for example, take a sledgehammer and smash it into kindling. Essential properties belong to the nature of a thing and cannot be changed or lost without altering the kind of thing it is. On the other hand, any change of a thing's nonessential properties would not change the kind of thing it is.

Many of the predicates applied to God denote not attributes or essential properties of God but nonessential properties that relate God to His creatures. Relational predicates like "creator," "ruler," and "preserver" do not denote divine attributes. A property like "being Lord of Israel" is likewise a nonessential property. It is logically possible that God might not have had this property. He might never have created Israel, or Israel might never have accepted Yahweh as its God. Being Lord of Israel is not essential to the being of God.

Once the essential properties of God are identified, one can be certain that any being lacking any of those essential properties could not be God. A being who lacks the essential property of omnipotence or omniscience or immutability would no longer qualify as a bearer of the title God. † If the being called God lost just one of His essential properties, He would no longer be God. A divine attribute then is a property that God could not lose and continue to be God. A divine attribute must be necessary to our idea of God.

An increasing number of contemporary philosophers are finding it helpful to approach some philosophical doctrines such as the theory of essential predication through the language of possible worlds. A possible world is a way the actual world could have been. The language of

---

†The argument of a later chapter will qualify this statement. Because some of the divine attributes are subject to significantly different interpretations, we may find it necessary to say that God is immutable in one sense and subject to change in another sense.

possible worlds is a handy way of referring to the possibility that things in the actual world might have been different. As absurd as it may seem, it is possible that the Cleveland Indians won the World Series in 1980. This possible but nonactual state of affairs can be referred to in terms of a possible world in which the Cleveland Indians won the 1980 World Series. To take a less incredible example, all manner of things are known about the Socrates who lived in the actual world: he was snub-nosed, he was married to Xanthippe, he was the teacher of Plato, he was a sculptor, and he was executed in 399 B.C. These propositions about Socrates would have to be included in any complete list of true propositions about the real world. But what if Socrates had not been snub-nosed or had not taught Plato or had not been executed? All these possibilities can be considered by suggesting possible worlds in which Socrates had a Roman nose or ran in the Olympic marathon or kicked Plato out of his class for cheating or died of old age. In other words, it is possible to imagine innumerable possible worlds in which Socrates exists that differ in some way from the real world.

How might the doctrine of essential predication be expressed in the semantics of possible worlds? One might state that the essence of an individual person is that set of properties he or she possesses in every possible world in which he or she exists. If there is any property that Socrates might not have in some possible world and still be Socrates, that property could not be part of his essence. Since it is possible that Socrates might not have been snub-nosed, snub-nosedness is obviously a nonessential property of Socrates. Any property that Socrates might have lacked in any possible world in which he exists could not be part of his essence. Both the author and reader of this page presumably have essential properties that characterize them in every possible world in which they exist. Presumably the amount of hair on their head or the color of their eyes is not part of that essence.

The terminology of possible worlds can now be used to define an attribute of God. A divine attribute is a property of God in every possible world in which God exists. Just as some being in a possible world who lacked Socrates' essence could not be Socrates, so a possible being who lacked one of the divine attributes could not be God, would not qualify as bearer of the title *God*. This means that God is omnipotent, omniscient, and so on in every possible world in which He exists.[12]

---

[12]A later chapter will consider the theory that God is a logically necessary being, which is to say that God exists in every possible world.

 Two
Concepts
of God

Much recent philosophical and theological literature reflects the struggle between two competing concepts of God. The contrasting theories are known by a variety of labels. The older, traditional view is frequently referred to simply as theism, often as Christian theism, sometimes as classical theism, and occasionally as Thomistic theism. The contemporary challenger goes by such names as panentheism, neoclassical theism, and Process theology. This chapter will explain the major differences between these two concepts of God, note some of the problems that attend each theory, and question the claim that the classical and neoclassical concepts of God are mutually exclusive alternatives.

THOMISTIC THEISM

In his book *God, Power and Evil: A Process Theodicy*,[1] David Ray Griffin presents an analysis of Thomistic or classical theism from his perspective as an advocate of Process theology. Though advocates of Thomistic theism may be unhappy with certain features of Griffin's presentation of their position, it offers some significant advantages for our study. For one thing, it presents in stark contrast the major differences between traditional theism (as it is understood by process thinkers) and panentheism. Even if Griffin's presentation should prove to be flawed or inaccurate in some respects, he succeeds in demonstrating the simple elegance of theism.

Griffin identifies a number of logically connected attributes which he calls "the essential core of theism." He believes this concept of God is a systematic explication of the theory found in Augustine and other classical theists who antedate Thomas Aquinas (1225–1274). To what

---

[1]David Ray Griffin, *God, Power and Evil: A Process Theodicy* (Philadelphia: Westminster, 1976).

extent the concept of God Griffin discusses deserves to be identified with classical Christian theism is an open question; but the package of attributes he identifies is sufficiently dependent on the writings of Thomas Aquinas to justify calling it the Thomistic concept of God. Griffin identifies eight attributes that make up the core of Thomistic theism: (1) pure actuality, (2) immutability, (3) impassibility, (4) time-lessness, (5) simplicity, (6) necessity, (7) omniscience, and, (8) omnipotence. Some readers will question the completeness of this list. What has happened, for example, to the attribute of divine love? Process theologians—Griffin and others—believe that properties like love, compassion, and sympathy are logically incompatible with the eight core attributes. In their view, one of the major tasks for Thomistic theism is showing how the God described in the Thomistic package of attributes can be the caring, loving God of the Bible.

The medieval doctrine of *actus purus* was the scholastic equivalent of Aristotle's teaching that God is pure actuality. Basic to the philosophy of Aristotle and his medieval followers was the belief that everything that exists is a combination of form and matter. Everything possesses both actuality and potentiality. (Of course, for Aristotle God is an exception to this. This is the whole point to his claim that God is pure form or actuality.) The form (essence) of a thing determines its actuality; its matter is the ground for the thing's several potentialities. While every existing thing can possess only one actuality at any given time, every existent possesses a number of different potentialities. Because of its essential properties, a given piece of wood, for example, may be in actuality a desk. But that same wood possesses the potentiality to be a number of different things, such as a chair or a table.

Aristotle regarded potentiality as a kind of imperfection. This conviction led him and Aquinas after him to believe that any potentiality in God's being would detract from His perfection.[2] Thus, it became easy for Christian thinkers who accepted this tradition to conclude that God must possess no potentiality; God must be pure actuality. While God can act, He cannot be acted upon. God therefore must be an exception to the doctrine that everything is composed of form and matter. Because potentiality cannot belong to God, God can possess no matter; He must be pure form.

Some of the implications that follow from Aristotle's doctrine of pure form are obviously difficult to reconcile with the Christian doctrine of God. For one thing, Aristotle taught that God cannot think about anything in the changing and imperfect world. The only perfect thing worthy of God's attention is God Himself. For Aristotle's God to think about anything else would detract from His perfection. Aristotle's

---

[2]For Aquinas's views on this point, see his *Summa Contra Gentiles* I.16.1.

Unmoved Mover whose only activity is contemplation of his own nature is a far cry from the loving God described in the Bible.

Two of the other attributes in Griffin's itemization of Thomistic theism, immutability, and impassibility, are related but not equivalent properties. Immutability suggests that God does not change, while impassibility refers to the impossibility of God's being acted upon. Impassibility also suggests that God cannot be "moved" in an emotional sense: God cannot be hurt, grieved, saddened, and so on. While Scripture sometimes speaks of God as subject to such emotions, many interpreters take these passages as metaphorical. As Griffin sees it, the attributes of immutability and impassibility conflict with passages in the Bible that speak of God changing His mind or being affected by the prayers of His people.

Griffin is convinced that Thomistic theism is required to interpret God's eternal existence as timelessness. True, most classical Christian theologians like Augustine and Aquinas understood God's eternity in the sense of timelessness. But the interpretation of Augustine and Aquinas need not be normative for subsequent generations of theists; nor does Griffin argue that it should be.[3] Attributing timelessness to God means more than saying that God's existence is without beginning or end. It means that God exists totally outside of time; that is, God has neither temporal duration nor temporal location. God does not exist at any particular moment of time and His existence does not occur during any period of time. He is "outside" of time. For a timeless God, all time exists in one eternal present; there is no past or future for God.

A number of Christian thinkers who are otherwise committed to classical Christian theism have had second thoughts about interpreting God's eternal existence as timelessness. They have preferred to say that God is everlasting. By this, they mean to say that while God has always existed and always will exist, it is a mistake to think of God as entirely divorced from the process of time. The debate as to which interpretation of God's eternity is correct holds significant implications for several areas of Christian doctrine. These questions will be considered in chapter 6.

The attribute of necessity is a double-barreled property. First, it implies that God's existence is necessary in the sense that it is impossible for God not to exist. Everything besides God exists contingently; that is, its nonexistence is possible. But if God exists, He exists necessarily; it is impossible that He might not have existed and it is impossible that He might cease to exist. The other dimension of the attribute of necessity

---

[3]Many contemporary theists find the notion of timelessness incompatible with the biblical picture of God. See Nicholas Wolterstorff's essay, "God Everlasting," in *God and the Good*, ed. Clifton Orlebeke and Lewis Smedes (Grand Rapids: Eerdmans, 1975).

deals with the relationship among the various attributes that make up the concept of God. The divine essence itself—the particular package of attributes God possesses—is necessary. In other words, it is not an accident that God possesses the attributes He does. It is in fact inescapable that God be the kind of being specified by the Thomistic package. There is nothing accidental or nonessential about the being of God.

Griffin thinks the attribute of simplicity may be the key to the Thomistic package since so much seems to follow from its attribution to God. If a being is simple, then it has no parts. If a being has no parts, then it cannot change (since there is nothing for it to lose or gain). If a thing cannot change (is immutable), then it must be pure actuality in the sense that it cannot possess any potentiality. "Before" and "after" would be inapplicable to such a being, a point which entails that any simple being must also be timeless. It would appear that the Thomistic concept of God cannot do without the property of simplicity.

The attributes of omnipotence and omniscience refer to God's power and knowledge respectively. As subsequent analysis will show, divine omnipotence does not mean, even for the Thomist, that God has the power to do absolutely everything. As a preliminary definition, divine omniscience means that God knows all truths and holds no false beliefs.

This then is one account of the influential classical concept of God that has played such an important role in the history of Christian theism. Thomists have usually believed that acceptance of any one attribute logically commits one to accepting the entire package. But if this has been one strength of the Thomistic concept of God, it may also prove in the present situation to be its Achilles' heel. A growing number of philosophers and theologians are persuaded that the Thomistic concept of God is fraught with serious problems. Moreover, these critics insist, because of the logical relationships among the attributes, no tinkering with the package is possible. Therefore, if the Thomistic concept of God really is inadequate, it must be abandoned in favor of a contemporary alternative such as Process theology. In the next section, the competing concept of God offered by Process theology will be examined. But it should be noted here that one is not forced to choose either Thomistic theism or Process theology; the disjunction between their respective theories of God is not exclusive. It is possible to develop mediating concepts of God that can avoid the major difficulties of the static God of Thomistic theism and the finite god of Process theology.

PROCESS THEOLOGY

Process theology takes its cue from three basic convictions. First, advocates of Process theology believe that the Thomistic concept of God cannot be delivered from a large number of serious objections. Second, they maintain that Christians should have been suspicious of the Thomistic package of attributes because of its heavy reliance upon ideas borrowed from pagan Greek philosophy and because of its alleged incompatibility with several major emphases of the Bible. Third, they believe that a much more satisfactory approach to the concept of God is to be found in the philosophy of the twentieth-century philosopher, Alfred North Whitehead.

Whitehead (1861–1947), son of an Anglican vicar, taught at Cambridge University and was for years best known for his work in the philosophy of science and the philosophy of mathematics. Between 1910 and 1913, he and Bertrand Russell co-authored the highly influential book *Principia Mathematica*. Whitehead eventually made his way to America and Harvard University where new interests began to develop at a fairly late stage in his career. His writings began to evidence a greater interest in speculative philosophy and traditional metaphysics. In books like his famous *Process and Reality*, he developed a metaphysical system in which the notion of process was paramount.

Whitehead's most influential interpreter, Charles Hartshorne (b. 1897), has himself written much that has stimulated the development of Process theology.[4] Other major proponents of the process system include Schubert Ogden,[5] John B. Cobb, Jr.,[6] Norman Pittenger,[7] Daniel Day Williams, Bernard Loomer, H. N. Wieman, David Ray Griffin, Peter Hamilton, and Ewert Cousins, among many others.[8]

Process theology views both pantheism and Thomistic theism as unacceptable extremes. In order to distinguish their position from pantheism, process theologians often call their theory panentheism. Whereas pantheism identifies God and the world in some way, panentheism denies that God and the world are identical. But while God and the world are not identical, they are interdependent, a claim that distinguishes panentheism from theism. Panentheists suggest that God be thought of as in the world much the way a mind is in a body. In fact, they often state, the world can be thought of as the body of God. Process theologians reject every one of the eight elements of the Thomistic

[4]Hartshorne has been a prolific writer. One place to begin a study of his thought is his book, *The Divine Relativity* (New Haven: Yale University Press, 1948).

[5]Schubert Ogden, *The Reality of God and Other Essays* (New York: Harper and Row, 1966).

[6]John B. Cobb, Jr., *A Christian Natural Theology* (Philadelphia: Westminster, 1965).

[7]Norman Pittenger, *Process Thought and Christian Faith* (New York: Macmillan, 1968).

[8]More general studies of the movement include: Delwin Brown, et al., *Process Philosophy and Christian Thought* (Indianapolis: Bobbs-Merrill, 1971); and Ewert Cousins, ed., *Process Theology* (New York: Newman, 1971). Both books contain helpful bibliographies.

package. They deny that God is pure actuality and they reject both the immutability and the impassibility of God. The God of Process theology is not outside of time; His existence is inextricably involved in the process of time. The process God is not simple. To the extent that the necessity of God is understood in the sense of aseity (God's independence from the world), this doctrine is rejected as well.* Process theologians make it clear that their God is neither omnipotent nor omniscient in any sense that would satisfy a traditional Christian theist. The process concept of God can be summarized in eleven theses which it offers in direct contrast to the tenets of Thomistic theism.[9]

1. In Process theology, Thomistic theism's emphasis upon *being* is replaced with its own stress upon *becoming*. According to process theologians, Thomistic theists view God as static and impassive substance. In process thought, substance is exchanged for process. Panentheists think of God and reality by means of models that stress interrelationship. One useful model for them is that of a society in which each component contributes something to the others. In a process universe, everything affects everything else—including God; the process God is no exception to this universal interdependence.

2. While the God of Christian theism is an independent Creator, the God of Process theology is an interdependent cooperator. Whether or not Christian theists accept the Thomist model in every respect, they believe that God is Creator. The doctrine of creation means that while the world is dependent upon God, God is not dependent on the world. Process theology denies God's independence of the world. For panentheism, God and the world are mutually dependent on each other. As Ewert Cousins explains:

> Aristotle views relation as involving change and dependence and hence imperfection. As a result, the Aristotelian-Thomistic school holds that the world can be related to God because it is dependent on him, but God cannot be really related to the world. If he were, then he would be dependent on creation and would not be the unmoved mover required by the Greek idea of perfection.[10]

Process thought, Cousins points out, opposes all such thinking.

The classical Christian doctrine of creation *ex nihilo* was one way early Christian thinkers marked off the ontological distance between

---

*It should be pointed out, however, that since some like Hartshorne are fervent defenders of the ontological argument, they insist that there is some sense in which God is a necessary being.

[9]Even though we shall frequently speak of *the* process concept of God, differences of opinion do exist within process thought. When those differences are important, attention will be drawn to them in the text or notes.

[10]Cousins, *Process Theology*, p. 15.

God and the world. They used this doctrine as a conscious repudiation of Plato's explanation of the origin of the world. In his *Timaeus*, Plato had taught that the world began when a finite god, much like an artist, fashioned the world out of pre-existing material. Christianity found Plato's view objectionable because it clearly limited the power and sovereignty of God. The process view of creation resembles Plato's to the extent that the Creation comes out of a pre-existent pole of God's own being. Whereas the classical Christian doctrine of creation implied God's control over the world, the God of process thought is not so much the controller of the world as He is its director. The process God works in the world;* He cooperates with the world. But He does not control the world: He is an interdependent partner with the world. For process theologians, neither God nor the world would be complete without the other. God's being has always been counterbalanced or complemented by things which exist independent of His will. The God of Process theology is not the sovereign Lord of the universe.

It follows then that process theologians also reject the traditional doctrine of divine transcendence. In classical Christian theology, God's transcendence was understood to mean His distinctness from the world. But the panentheist belief that the world is God's body rules out the notion of transcendence.

3. The classical Christian doctrine of divine immutability is replaced by the notion of a changing God. Process thinkers attempt to support their rejection of divine immutability by appealing to the biblical picture of God. How, they ask, could a totally unchanging God respond to the prayers of His people? For this reason, Cousins believes that the God of process thought

> is closer to the Christian experience and to the Biblical witness than is the timeless Absolute of Greek philosophy. For the Christian God is concerned with the world; he is involved in its suffering and its tragedy. The world, man, and human events make a difference to him. The deepest reality of God is seen not in his detachment or in his power, but in his love. In contrast with the static Absolute and the all-powerful monarch, the process God is the God of persuasive love revealed in Jesus Christ.[11]

Process theologians stress the apparent incompatibility between the biblical view of God as truly personal and the classical emphasis on immutability and impassiveness. The impassive God of scholastic philosophy, they say, is inconsistent with the biblical God who is personal, loving, and caring.

---

*Theism, of course, through its doctrine of divine immanence, also affirms that God is active in the world. But it rejects the interdependence between God and the world that is such an important element of process thought.

[11]Cousins, *Process Theology*, p. 15.

4. In the writings of some process thinkers, the personal God of theism appears to be replaced by an impersonal God. This is a point of major disagreement among process thinkers. It is unlikely that White-head's God can be regarded as personal since his God was not really distinct from other beings. The personal character of Pittenger's God is also debatable. According to Pittenger, while God is the ground of the personal, he nevertheless transcends personal categories. Other process thinkers, however, like John Cobb, Jr., attempt to allow for a view of God as a living person.[12]

5. Process theologians unanimously reject the timelessness doctrine of Thomistic theism. They believe "it is self-contradictory to think of God as both alive and changeless. If God is alive, then he must experience some change. And this means that God literally experiences and exemplifies process. That is, he enjoys the experience of before and after. He is everlasting and omnitemporal, but not timeless."[13] Instead of being timeless, God is "temporal, relative, dependent, and constantly changing."[14] It is important to note, however, that the dispute over divine timelessness is not unique to process thinkers. An increasing number of classical theists find a reinterpretation of God's relationship to time compatible with other elements of their concept of God.

6. While both theists and panentheists describe God as perfect, representatives of the two movements understand perfection in significantly different ways. For classical theists, God's perfection means (among other things) that nothing more can be added to God's being: He is complete or fulfilled perfection. For the panentheist, however, God's perfection is being attained successively; God is continually growing or developing in perfection. As the amount of value within the universe (God's body) increases, God's own perfection evolves and grows. As Ewert Cousins states:

> Classical theism applied to God the Greek notion of perfection, claiming that God is absolutely perfect in all respects and in no way surpassable. In Hartshorne's view, God is perfect in love, in goodness, in the omnipresence and the omnicompetence of his sensitivity to the world. But his perfection must be defined in such a way that it includes the possibility of his self-surpassing experience of new value. This involves some limitations on classical doctrines of perfection, especially on omnipotence.[15]

7. Theists and panentheists disagree as to whether God should be

---

[12]See Cobb's *Natural Theology*, pp. 188f.
[13]J. E. Barnhart, *Religion and the Challenge of Philosophy* (Totowa, N.J.: Littlefield, Adams and Co., 1975), p. 153.
[14]John Cobb, Jr., and David Ray Griffin, *Process Theology: An Introductory Exposition* (Philadelphia: Westminster, 1976), p. 47.
[15]Cousins, *Process Theology*, p. 14.

understood as absolute or relative. "Absolute" in this context means that God cannot be involved in any *real* relationship with the world. "Relative" carries with it the notion of being related to something, in this case, being related to the world. Traditional theism affirms that while God gives meaning to the world, it is impossible for the world to give any meaning to God. Process thinkers disagree. God needs the world, they maintain, in order to "enrich his everlasting existence and to give it stimulus and meaning, as well as 'embodiment.'"[16]

To state that God needs some world is not to say that He needs this particular world or the particular creatures in this world. He might be able to get along just as well with a different world. But God does need some world to complement His existence. Process thinkers insist that God actually receives something from the world; the world adds something to God, something which He would otherwise lack. According to Lewis Ford, if God's experience were not actually enriched by the world, "the existence of the world would be wholly gratuitous, devoid of any ultimate significance."[17] Since God includes all experiences within His own being, the finite creatures who exist within God "are not simply the passive effects of God but are also *causes* having an impact on one another and consequently on or in God."[18]

Process thinkers, however, give little attention to the apparent equivocation in their position on this subject. Even if God is related to everything that exists, how does it follow that God is therefore relative? Recognizing this, Schubert Ogden has admitted that God's "being related to all others is itself relative to nothing, but the absolute ground of any and all real relationships."[19]

8. Another disagreement between theism and panentheism concerns the question whether God's omniscience is unqualified or restricted. Theists have traditionally viewed God as omniscient in the strong sense: God knows all things including future contingent actions. Since God's knowledge is complete, there is no sense in which it can be said to grow. Process thinkers like Hartshorne explain God's knowledge as a process of God becoming aware of the experiences and knowledge of the creatures who exist within His own being. Because God knows all of the past and present experiences of such creatures, because His own being encompasses all such entities and their experiences, Hartshorne's God is omniscient with respect to all past and present events. But for

---

[16]Barnhart, *Religion and the Challenge of Philosophy*, p. 153.

[17]Lewis S. Ford, "The Viability of Whitehead's God for Christian Theology," *Proceedings of the American Catholic Philosophical Association* 44 (1970): 148.

[18]Barnhart, *Religion and the Challenge of Philosophy*, p. 152.

[19]Schubert Ogden, "Love Unbounded: The Doctrine of God," *Perkins School of Theology Journal* 19 (1966): 14.

Hartshorne, it is impossible for even God to have knowledge about the future. The future is open and indeterminate and not even God can know it.

9. Traditional theism emphasizes God's role as efficient cause of the world; process thought stresses God's role as final cause. In other words, God, who is the goal or lure of the entire cosmic process, draws it to its final fulfillment. God is the final cause or *telos* of the world. But process theologians are wrong if they think it would be inconsistent for a theist to maintain that God is both the efficient *and* the final cause of the world.

10. In a sense, the foundation-for most of the distinctive doctrines of Process theology is its insistence that the monopolar notion of God found in traditional theism should be replaced by a dipolar view of God. The monopolar view of God conceives of God as absolutely perfect: His absoluteness is unqualified. But according to Hartshorne, God should be thought of as comprising two contrasting poles. The dipolar view originated with Whitehead who regarded the world as the *actual pole* of God. But, Whitehead insisted, if the world were all there is to God, the result would be pantheism. And so, he held, there is also a *potential pole* to God's being which is beyond the world. With respect to His potentiality, God is absolute, eternal, and infinite. With respect to His actual pole (the world), God is relative, temporal, and finite. God's *primordial nature* (the potential pole) is what God is eternally; God's *consequent nature* (or His actual nature) is what God is at any given moment. As Hartshorne interprets the doctrine, the two natures or poles of God are as follows:

God's Primordial Nature	God's Consequent Nature
abstract	concrete
necessary	contingent
transcendent	immanent
eternal	temporal
potential	actual
one	many
infinite	finite
cause	effect
absolute	relative
immutable	mutable

Whitehead expressed this dipolar characteristic of God by writing:

It is as true to say that God is permanent and the World fluent, as that the world is permanent and God is fluent.

It is as true to say that God is one and the World many, as that the World is one and God many. . . .

It is as true to say that the World is immanent in God, as that God is immanent in the World.

It is as true to say that God transcends the World, as that the World transcends God.

It is as true to say that God creates the World, as that the World creates God.[20]

The primordial pole of God can be thought of as the mind of God; it is akin to Plato's realm of eternal objects. The consequent or actual pole is the sum total of everything that exists at any given moment. The two poles can be thought of as representing God's mind and His body. The eternal objects of God's primordial nature lack an independent existence; they are potentialities which may or may not come to be actualized in the universe. Until they are actualized, the eternal objects exist only as concepts in the minds of such actual entities as God. Therefore, God's primordial nature can be viewed as an envisagement of all the possibilities which could someday become actual.

The dipolar God is involved in an endless process of change. Everything that exists is in a continual state of process; it is constantly becoming something else through its interaction with other entities. God contributes permanence to temporal beings while temporal beings dispense flux to God. God's source of diversity is the world and the world's source of unity is God. "Creativity" is the process thinker's name for the all-encompassing process. The concrete pole of God's being, the world, describes, for some particular moment of the process, what God is. Therefore, the world is the physical realization or actualization of God's conceptual vision. No contradiction is supposed to exist between the two poles of God's being since they describe different aspects of God.

11. The final difference between theism and panentheism to be noted here is their attitude to the question of God's ultimate triumph over evil. Traditional theism affirms the ultimate victory of God over all forms of evil; panentheism, sometimes with regret, disagrees. According to panentheism, no ultimate triumph over evil is possible for God. Evil can never be completely conquered or destroyed. Barnhart admits: "No claim is made that God can guarantee that Christians or any other group will enjoy everlasting personal victory over all suffering and death."[21]

The eleven points I have noted draw attention to the major ways in which the God of Process theology differs from the God of classical

---

[20]Alfred North Whitehead, *Process and Reality* (New York: Harper and Row, 1960 reprint), p. 528. Not all process theologians accept a dipolar view of God. John Cobb, Jr., for one, denies the doctrine; see his *A Christian Natural Theology*, pp. 176ff.

[21]Barnhart, *Religion and the Challenge of Philosophy*, p. 151.

theism. But my treatment of theism in this section has been tinged with some ambiguity. It is now time to deal with this equivocation. Throughout this section, I have referred to theism in a variety of ways. Sometimes, I contrasted Process theology with the distinctive package of attributes earlier attributed to Thomistic theism. At other times, I referred more generally to something called classical or traditional theism. Much of the influence Process theology has gained in the last forty years is a result of its claim that Thomistic theism and classical theism are identical. While there is undoubtedly some overlap, I wish to contest the claim of identity. Is the Thomistic package of attributes that was described earlier in this chapter normative for any Christian theism that desires to be faithful to the Scriptures as well as to the orthodox creeds of the church? I think this is still an open question.

Because process thinkers have equated Thomistic theism with traditional Christian theism, they have maintained that responsible Christians have only two choices; they are confronted by an either/or situation. A Christian must either adopt the entire Thomistic package of attributes or else reject the Thomistic concept of God and accept the process view of God. Supposedly, there is no third alternative. Once people accept the view that only two choices are available, and begin to see the serious problems that attend the Thomistic theory of God, the appeal of the process package increases immensely. There is only one slight catch to all this. The disjunction, either Thomistic theism or panentheism, is not exclusive. There are other alternatives. It may be best to think of Thomistic theism and Process theology as opposite poles of a continuum along which a variety of other alternatives can be found. Rejection of the Thomistic package as described earlier in the chapter does not necessarily require one to accept the process concept of God.

SOME PROBLEMS WITH PROCESS THEOLOGY

Either Thomistic theism or panentheism: We have already seen that this is a forced and artificial choice. Even if Thomistic theism is found unacceptable, panentheism is not the only alternative. Many process thinkers seem to be drawn into this forced choice by their uncritical identification of the God of theism with Aristotle's Unmoved Mover, who was unrelated to the world, impassive, and unconcerned. But as Bruce Demarest argues:

> The Christian faith emerged out of the matrix of Judaism with its conception of God as a living, active being relentlessly operative in the ordinary events of nature and the supernatural display of miracles. The God of the Jewish-Christian tradition is changeless in being, attributes and purposes, but in His dealings with the creation God does enter into changing relations. Thus, the divine immutability in no wise implies that God is

unconcerned, inactive, or unrelated. . . . It is wholly irresponsible to replace the God of theism with a finite, evolving Deity in order to affirm relatedness to the world. Biblical faith unhesitatingly affirms that the perfection of God includes creative interaction consistent with His changeless character and purposes.[22]

Traditional theists like Demarest maintain then that God's perfection does not preclude but rather includes relations with His creation. The recognition of this fact does not conflict with the belief that God's character and purposes are unchanging.

Especially ironic is the oft-recurring panentheist claim that Thomistic theism is dominated to an inordinate degree by the influence of pagan Greek philosophy. Perhaps this is true. But it is just as true that Process theology is equally indebted to ancient Greek thought; it simply elevates a different Greek tradition to prominence. The conflict between Thomistic theism and Process theology is basically a revival of the struggle between competing schools of Greek philosophy, one emphasizing *being*, the other stressing the dominance of *becoming*. A process theologian chiding a Thomist for his dependence on Greek thought is like the pot calling the kettle black.

Equally ironic is the effort process theologians expend trying to make it appear that their position is more consistent with the teaching of Holy Scripture than is the position of the Thomistic theist. Since the process theologian himself introduces faithfulness to Scripture as a criterion of theological adequacy, it is legitimate to inquire about the extent to which Process theology itself satisfies this test. Most process theologians appear to have a highly selective biblical hermeneutic. Scripture is welcomed as authoritative when it agrees with panentheist opinions. But when Scripture conflicts with cherished beliefs, it is conveniently ignored or casually discarded.

Critics of Process theology frequently express reservations about its doctrine of Christ. And in the writings of process thinkers, their rejection of the deity of Jesus Christ comes across clearly.[23] Hartshorne readily acknowledges, "I have no Christology to offer, beyond the simple suggestion that Jesus appears to be the supreme symbol furnished to us by history of the notion of God genuinely and literally 'sympathetic' . . . receiving into his own experience the sufferings as well as the joys of the world."[24] Some process thinkers disassociate themselves

---

[22]Bruce Demarest, "Process Trinitarianism," in *Perspectives on Evangelical Theology*, ed. Kenneth S. Kantzer and Stanley N. Gundry (Grand Rapids: Baker, 1979), p. 29.

[23]For examples, see Cobb, *Christ in a Pluralistic Age* (Philadelphia: Westminster, 1975), pp. 74ff., or Pittenger, *Christology Reconsidered* (London: SCM, 1970), p. 79.

[24]Charles Hartshorne, *Reality as Social Process: Studies in Metaphysics and Religion* (Boston: Beacon, 1953), p. 24.

from Hartshorne's position on the grounds that Hartshorne himself recognizes how his theological convictions differ from traditional Christian teachings. But even the Christian theologians within the movement make it clear that their christology is a radical reinterpretation of traditional dogma. Cobb and Griffin admit that "Process theology is not interested in formulating distinctions within God for the sake of conforming with traditional Trinitarian notions."[25]

Nor does Process theology line up any better with a host of other basic Christian beliefs: the Incarnation, the bodily Resurrection, the Atonement. Traditional Catholics and Protestants deplore the extent to which process thinkers cut the ties to the historic Christian faith and in effect offer the world a distinctly new religion. If process theologians disqualify Thomism on scriptural grounds, they cannot ignore Scripture as a possible ground for disqualifying Process theology. To the extent that process theologians present their position as an expression of *Christian* thought, the fidelity of their views to the normative documents of the Christian faith is a valid consideration. It is certainly a point at which they have major problems.

But Process theology has philosophical problems as well. Many critics have sensed that a major difficulty lies somewhere within panentheism's dipolar view of God. One writer who struggled to make this problem explicit was Thomist theologian E. L. Mascall. He noted that Whitehead, to cite just one example, "has concentrated his thought so thoroughly upon the *way in which things behave* as never really to inquire *why they are*. He has never properly understood what finite being *is* and so has never apprehended its radical contingency."[26] Mascall seems to be saying that the dipolar God of process thought deprives the process theologian of any answer to the question, *why* does the actual world exist? Since the potential nature of God is eternal, it is easy enough to grant that the realm of potentialities requires no sufficient reason for its existence. But the things that exist within the actual world (the consequent nature of God) are contingent.[27] Why do these con-

---

[25]Cobb and Griffin, *Process Theology*, p. 110. It is sometimes said by panentheists that their doctrine of eternal creation (or actuality) and their rejection of the traditional doctrine of creation *ex nihilo* protects the doctrine of God's eternal relatedness and sociality: God always has some (created) reality to relate to. But a strong doctrine of the Trinity would protect the sociality doctrine far more biblically and classically. And Trinity doctrine is strangely neglected in process thought—or else, as in the case of Pittenger, just reduced to a form of modalism.

[26]E. L. Mascall, *He Who Is* (London: Longmans, Green and Co., 1962), p. 158.

[27]An important distinction is necessary at this point. Panentheists allow that the world as such can be eternal in the sense that God may have always had a body. But even if the world itself is eternal, the particular things within the world are not. And as contingent beings, they require a sufficient reason for their existence.

tingent things, these particulars that happen to be exist? Why were some potentialities actualized and not others? Mascall says,

> we still want to know why [existing finite things] are there at all. To say that they are units of Creativity explains nothing, unless we are also told why they are the particular units that they are, manifesting the particular kinds of Creativity that they do. The one thing that they are clearly not is self-explanatory, but this is the one fact that Whitehead never allows himself to think about. He postulates God as the ground of rationality, but never as the ground of being.[28]

In short, Whitehead and other process thinkers develop a metaphysical system that leaves unanswered the most fundamental of all metaphysical questions, why is there anything at all? It is a system of explanation that fails to provide any ultimate explanation.

Another Thomist, Norman Geisler, picks up the same point and takes it in a slightly different direction. Geisler argues that

> if God has both an actual pole and a potential pole, one is faced with disturbing metaphysical questions. How can God actualize his own potentialities? Potentialities cannot actualize themselves any more than empty cups can fill themselves. Capacities do not fulfill themselves; they must be activated by something outside themselves. Anything passing from potentiality to actuality, from what is not to what is, depends on some actuality to ground it. Nothing does not produce something; possibilities to exist do not materialize on their own.[29]

The point is that in process thought, God's eternal and potential nature is given. But then, in some way, some of God's infinite potentialities are actualized in the things that make up the concrete world which is also God's consequent nature. Geisler wants some explanation of how those potentialities become actualities. After all, potentialities do not have the power to actualize themselves; if they did, they would be something other than potentialities.

Much the same concern is felt by W. Norris Clarke who suggests that Whitehead's dipolar view of God and rejection of the Christian doctrine of creation out of nothing

> brings us back to an older Platonic primal dualism of God over against the world . . . where neither of these two primal poles is ultimately responsible for the other. What then is the ultimate source or explanation of the unity of the universe, of why its two correlative poles, God and the

---

[28]Mascall, *He Who Is*, p. 159.

[29]Norman Geisler, *Christian Apologetics* (Grand Rapids: Baker, 1976), pp. 208–9. Compare also the following comment by William J. Hill: "How can anything that lacks all actuality function as the explanatory Principle of the fact that there *are* finite instances of actuality (that there are beings rather than nothing)?" William J. Hill, "In What Sense Is God Infinite? A Thomistic Perspective," *The Thomist* 42 (1978): 20.

multiplicity of the world, are attuned to each other so as to make up a single system, since neither one ultimately derives all of its being from the other? If there is to be any ultimate source of unity in the universe at all—which is dubious, just as it was for Plato—it seems to be pushed back beyond even God to an inscrutable, faceless, amorphous force of creativity which is just *there*, everywhere in the universe, as a primal fact with no further explanation possible—a kind of generalized necessity of nature, with striking similarities to the ancient Greek *ananke*. [30]

In response to the kinds of questions raised by Mascall and Geisler, many process thinkers do exactly what Clarke notices: they appeal to something they call creativity in order to explain what makes it possible for God to actualize His own potentialities. But this move appears to raise even more serious problems for the panentheist. Geisler explains:

> It is self-destructive to the [panentheistic] system to posit something like Whitehead's "creativity" with reality status outside the bipolar actual entities of the world. Only actual entities actually exist in the world, and beyond the world only potentialities exist, namely, eternal objects. Creativity cannot be a real ground in a Whiteheadian system; only actual entities are real causes. [31]

Dipolar theism starts out with a system in which everything is either an actual entity that concretely exists in the world or one of the eternal potentialities existing in the primordial nature of God. But this dualism excludes anything that can serve as a sufficient reason for the existence of any actual entity. When a solution to the problem is sought by appealing to something else called creativity, the original dipolar emphasis of panentheism is effectively abandoned and a third thing, whatever creativity turns out to be, is held to exist outside the world. But this appears to elevate creativity above God.

> Should a panentheist wish to revise the Whiteheadian system by giving a reality status to something beyond God in which he [God] is grounded, then his "God" turns out not to be God after all. For if there is a real creative ground for the bipolar "God," then it is this pure actuality beyond the bipolar potentiality-actuality that is really God. In short, panentheism needs a theistic God in order to ground its "God," which turns out after all

[30]W. Norris Clarke, S.J., *The Philosophical Approach to God* (Winston-Salem, N.C.: Wake Forest University Publications, 1979), p. 72.

[31]Geisler, *Christian Apologetics*, p. 209. For additional discussions of problems related to the notion of creativity, see Robert C. Neville, "Whitehead on the One and the Many," *The Southern Journal of Philosophy* 7 (1969–70): 391ff., and David L. Schindler, "Creativity as Ultimate: Reflections on Actuality in Whitehead, Aristotle, and Aquinas," *International Philosophical Quarterly* 13 (1973): 161–71.

not to be God but to be a giant creature needing a more ultimate and real cause of itself.[32]

In other words, attempts to explain why actual entities exist which appeal to Whitehead's "creativity" seem to end in an appeal to something that is more ultimate than the dipolar God. Thus, the rationality of the dipolar system seems to depend on a more ultimate monopolar principle.

For Bruce Demarest, the dipolar God of process thought is a hoax or mirage. Echoing some of the points already made, he charges: "The primordial pole of God, which possesses no actuality, in fact possesses no reality. The attempt to impose upon the system a transcendent, timeless anchor in the form of the primordial nature smacks of a desperate attempt to forestall the system's collapse into radical immanentism and pantheism."[33] Demarest regards dipolar theism not as a brilliant stroke of genius, but as a desperate act of expediency. Without it, panentheism would have nothing to prevent its inevitable collapse into sheer pantheism.

One additional problem with Process theology has been noted, and deserves brief attention. Because of panentheism's unmitigated stress upon the change and process that characterizes everything including God, it is difficult to see how the God of process thought can retain any identity. A long and honored tradition in philosophy holds that if something retains identity through time, there must be something about it that is the same, that remains unchanged. But since in process thought God is totally subject to the vicissitudes of change, nothing can possibly ground His identity. What reason then have Christians today to believe that the God they worship is the *same* God worshiped by Moses and revealed by Jesus Christ?

As we shall see in the next section, Thomistic theism has its own problems. Some of those difficulties have driven many sincere and conscientious people into the arms of panentheism. It is interesting to speculate whether the problems they left behind are really less severe than the ones that now confront them.

SOME PROBLEMS WITH THOMISTIC THEISM

Since several of the problems generated by Thomistic theism will be discussed in later chapters, my present diagnosis of its ills can be comparatively short. Many traditional theists concur with a number of criticisms directed by process theologians against the Thomistic concept

---

[32]Geisler, *Christian Apologetics*, p. 209. Other attacks on dipolar theism and its appeal to creativity can be found in Robert C. Neville, *Creativity and God* (New York: Seabury, 1980) and W. Norris Clarke, *The Philosophical Approach to God*, pp. 72ff.

[33]Demarest, "Process Trinitarianism," p. 29.

of God. They believe, for example, that panentheism is correct when it recognizes the importance of God's real and significant relationship with the world. Norman Geisler, a philosopher who usually sides with Aquinas, readily acknowledges that a God

> who cannot act or interact with the world would be less than significantly personal. Prayer and service possess little meaning unless there is a real, personal relationship between God and men. The God of the Bible and of Christian experience is responsive to human needs and actions. There is no existential appeal in an impersonal and unrelatable Being. The doctrine of God's relationality is a biblical and vital teaching which is neglected or lost in some expressions of traditional theism.[34]

Geisler also acknowledges that the Greek approach to God that viewed deity in exclusively essentialist categories distorts the biblical view of God. He thinks panentheism is correct when it

> points up the need to explain the dynamic God of Christian revelation in more than purely static essentialistic Greek categories. The God of the Judaeo-Christian Scriptures is more than a static unchangeable Essence or a platonic Super-Form; he is a personal God of ceaseless creative activity. He actively sustains the creative world process. He is active in history and manifest in nature. To explain the Christian God in pure Greek categories of Being is to dress him up in the straight-jacket of essentialism, rather than to see him in the light of his dynamic and changing actions and interpersonal relationships.[35]

Without question, several panentheist objections to certain features of the Thomistic package of attributes express legitimate concerns.

In each of the chapters that follow, we will look more closely at a particular attribute from among those that make up the essential core of Thomistic theism. In addition to clarifying the meaning of the attributes, I will seek to determine what modifications in our understanding of the attributes may be necessary to answer those who claim that single attributes are incoherent or that inconsistency exists within the set of properties that make up the Thomistic concept of God. And, of course, I will seek a mediating concept of God that would preserve the legitimate concerns while avoiding the most serious difficulties of both the process and the Thomistic concepts of God.

[34]Norman Geisler, "Process Theology," in *Tensions in Contemporary Theology*, ed. Stanley N. Gundry and Alan F. Johnson (Chicago: Moody, 1976), p. 268.

[35]Geisler, *Christian Apologetics*, p. 208.

 Omnipotence

Anyone who has attempted to define satisfactorily the attribute of omnipotence knows how difficult this is. It is comforting to know that even Thomas Aquinas encountered problems here: While "all confess that God is omnipotent . . . it seems difficult to explain in what His omnipotence precisely consists."[1] Anthony Kenny concurs: "It is by no means easy to state concisely and coherently what is meant by 'omnipotence.'"[2]

Some thinkers apparently believe that any limitations (logical or otherwise) upon the power of God seriously undermine the classical claim that God is omnipotent. This explains why many people suggest that divine omnipotence means God can do anything. But if there is anything to be learned from the classical Christian discussions of omnipotence, it is that omnipotence was always understood to be compatible with certain limitations upon God's power. There are certain things that even an omnipotent God cannot do.

Medieval theologians drew attention to some fairly trivial examples of restrictions upon the power of God. How could God be called omnipotent, for example, when He could not do some things that His creatures could do, such as walk, sit, or swim? The standard scholastic answer suggested that such creaturely acts did not mean that humans possessed powers not possessed by God. Rather, human acts such as walking and swimming were possible because of a defect in human power. The ability to sin, for example, is not a power but a defect or infirmity. The ability to walk results from having a body—also, in their

[1]Thomas Aquinas, *Summa Theologica*, trans. the Fathers of the English Dominican Province, vol. 1 (New York: Benziger Brothers, 1947), 137. This and all of the quotations from Aquinas in this chapter (3) are from part I, question 25, articles 3 and 4 of the *Summa*.

[2]Anthony Kenny, *The God of the Philosophers* (Oxford: Clarendon, 1979), p. 91.

view, a defect. As the discussion of omnipotence progressed through the Middle Ages, Christian philosophers came to qualify the statement "God can do anything" by adding "that implies the perfection of true power." As Aquinas phrased it, "God is said to be omnipotent in respect to active power, not to passive power."

OMNIPOTENCE AND THE LAWS OF LOGIC

Something may be said to be possible or impossible in two distinct ways: *physical possibility* or *logical possibility*. Most Christian thinkers have followed Aquinas in holding that logical consistency—not merely physical possibility—is a necessary condition for divine omnipotence.[3] In the first sense, physical possibility, something is possible for any being if he possesses the power to do it. If someone has the power to lift three hundred pounds, for example, then obviously the act of lifting three hundred pounds is physically possible for *that* person. Some acts (like running a mile in thirty seconds or swimming across the Atlantic) do not appear to be physically possible for any human being. Aquinas realized that nothing can be gained from analyzing divine omnipotence in terms of physical possibility. In his words, if "we were to say that God is omnipotent because He can do all things that are possible to His power, there would be a vicious circle in explaining the nature of His power. For this would be saying nothing else but that God is omnipotent because He can do all that He is able to do."

The more promising approach to an explanation of divine omnipotence, Aquinas thought, lay in the second type of possibility, logical possibility. Something is possible in the logical sense if it does not violate the law of noncontradiction. As Aquinas put it, "Everything that does not imply a contradiction is numbered among those possibles in respect of which God is called omnipotent; whereas whatever implies contradiction does not come within the scope of divine omnipotence, because it cannot have the aspect of possibility. Hence it is more appropriate to say that such things cannot be done, than that God cannot do them." Any act that is logically impossible must also be physically impossible. Squaring the circle is both logically and physically impossible. Aquinas denied that the exclusion of logically impossible acts from the sphere of divine power constituted any limitation on God's power. He regarded logically impossible tasks as pseudo-tasks. A being's inability to perform a pseudo-task (for example, creating a square circle) cannot count against its power. Thus logical possibility, as Aquinas saw it, is a necessary though not a sufficient condition for any exercise of God's power.

René Descartes and a few other philosophers have rejected the

---

[3]*Summa Theologica* I, 25, 3.

view that God's power is limited by the law of noncontradiction. Descartes believed an omnipotent being could do absolutely anything including that which is self-contradictory: God's actions are not limited by the laws of logic. Descartes advanced this view on the conviction, apparently, that the Thomist position dishonors God by making Him subject to a law (the law of noncontradiction) that Descartes believed is as dependent on God's will as any other law. Just as God could have created the world so that it was governed by different laws of nature, so also He could have subjected the world to different logical and mathematical laws. According to Descartes, God freely decreed the logical and mathematical truths that obtain in our world and could have created a different world in which the principle of noncontradiction or propositions like *"two plus two equals four"* were necessarily false.

The first thing that should be noted about Descartes's position is that it is unassailable. Since any sound argument or refutation must begin by presupposing certain rules, it is impossible to argue against someone who rejects the most basic rules of reasoning. J. L. Mackie observes that anyone holding Descartes's view

> need never be disturbed by any reasoning or any evidence, for if his omnipotent being could do what is logically impossible, he could certainly exist, and have any desired attributes, in defiance of every sort of contrary consideration. The view that there is an absolutely omnipotent being in this sense stands, therefore, right outside the realm of rational enquiry and discussion; once held, it is so unassailable that it is a waste of time to consider it further.[4]

Thus, it is unlikely that committed believers in Descartes's position will be persuaded by any argument. Still, several points are worth making. Those who affirm that God can do anything and who also accept the authority of Scripture, must deal with Scripture's own assertions that there are things God cannot do. God cannot lie, for example, or swear by a being greater than Himself (Heb. 6:18, 13). Scripture does not view the power of God as the unqualified ability to do absolutely anything. The catch, of course, is that such an *ad hominem* argument only points out an inconsistency in those who believe that God can do anything and who also believe the Scriptures are true. A determined irrationalist may reply that since logical inconsistency does not bother God, it does not trouble him either.

Several philosophers and theologians have pointed out the absurdity of regarding a self-contradictory description as *some thing*. Richard Swinburne, for example, argues that those who think a truly omnipo-

---

[4] J. L. Mackie, "Omnipotence," *Sophia* 1 (1962): 16. Mackie's article along with other relevant discussions is reprinted in *The Power of God*, ed. Linwood Urban and Douglas N. Walton (New York: Oxford University Press, 1978), pp. 73–88.

tent being ought to be able to do the logically impossible err because they regard

> a logically impossible action as an action of one kind on a par with an action of another kind, the physically impossible. But it is not. A logically impossible action is not an action. It is what is described by a form of words which purport to describe an action, but do not describe anything which it is coherent to suppose could be done. It is no objection to A's omnipotence that he cannot make a square circle. This is because "making a square circle" does not describe anything which it is coherent to suppose could be done.[5]

J. L. Mackie, hardly a friend of theism, agrees that nothing in this problem should count against the coherence of the attribute of omnipotence or the plausibility of Theism:

> A logical contradiction is not a state of affairs which it is supremely difficult to produce, but only a form of words which fails to describe any state of affairs. So to say, as we are now saying, that "God is omnipotent" means "God can do or make to be X, for any X provided that doing X or making X to be is not logically impossible" would be to say that if God is omnipotent every coherently describable activity or production is within his power.[6]

A logical contradiction can at most describe a pseudo-task. And God's inability to perform a pseudo-task cannot count against His omnipotence. As Aquinas noted, it is better to state that such pseudo-tasks cannot be done, period, than to say that God cannot do them.

A supralogical God would be unknowable and unintelligible. Whatever God's relation to the laws of logic may be, it is clear that all human thinking and communication must presuppose the law of noncontradiction. "As we cannot say how a nonlogical world would look, we cannot say how a supralogical God would act or how He would communicate anything to us by way of revelation."[7] A supralogical God is a God about whom nothing can be said or known.

Moreover, a supralogical God would introduce devastating implications into any religion promoting such a concept. If God can do self-contradictory acts, then there is no inconsistency in His *promising* eternal life to all who trust in Christ but actually condemning to everlasting damnation all who trust Christ. Such duplicity (inconsistency) would be entirely in character for a God not bound by the law of noncontradiction since, in a world where the law does not apply, there

---

[5]Richard Swinburne, *The Coherence of Theism* (Oxford: Clarendon Press, 1977), p. 149.

[6]Mackie, "Omnipotence," p. 16.

[7]Peter Geach, *Providence and Evil* (New York: Cambridge University Press, 1977), p. 11.

is no difference between eternal life and eternal damnation. But if there is a difference, if things are what they are and not their contradictory, then the law of noncontradiction holds. The specter that accompanies Descartes's concept of God is the possibility of God saying, "I know I promised eternal life to all who believe in Jesus but I see no inconsistency in repudiating that promise and awarding eternal life to all who rejected Jesus." This is only a sample of the absurdities that defenders of a supralogical God must be prepared to accept.

CAN GOD SIN?

The discussion about the relationship between omnipotence and logic makes it clear that omnipotence does not include the ability to do everything. There are limits even to what an omnipotent being can do. Some medieval thinkers raised another possible problem with respect to omnipotence. They wondered if God can sin. Suppose we grant that an omnipotent God can do anything that is logically possible. Sinning is an act that is both logically and physically possible. After all, human beings do it all the time. How then can God be omnipotent if He cannot sin? Both Anselm and Thomas Aquinas appear to have advanced similar answers to the question. "But how art Thou omnipotent," Anselm asked,

> if Thou art not capable of all things? or, if Thou canst not be corrupted and canst not lie . . . how art Thou capable of all things? Or else to be capable of these things is not power but impotence. For he who is capable of those things is capable of what is not for his good, and of what he ought not to do and the more capable of them he is, the more power have adversity and perversity against him; and the less has he himself against these.[8]

Anselm thought the question important because the claim that God cannot sin appears to be incompatible with the assertion of His omnipotence. Anselm's suggested solution pointed out that the ability to sin results not from power but from a lack of power. Aquinas argued similarly that "to sin is to fall short of a perfect action; hence to be able to sin is to be able to fall short in action, which is repugnant to omnipotence. Therefore, it is that God cannot sin, because of his omnipotence."[9] The point that Anselm and Aquinas were trying to make is elusive and requires some effort to grasp. Some progress toward understanding their position may be gained by studying the more detailed discussion of the eighteenth-century theologian, Samuel Clarke (1675–1729).

Clarke began by acknowledging that God "must of necessity have

---

[8]Anselm, *Proslogium*, chapter 7; cited from S. N. Deane, *St. Anselm* (La Salle, Illinois: Open Court, 1958), p. 14.

[9]Aquinas, *Summa Theologica* I, 25, 3, p. 138.

infinite power. This proposition is evident and undeniable."[10] Since God's infinite power cannot be denied, "the only question is, what the true meaning of what we call infinite power is, and to what things it must be understood to extend, or not to extend." Clarke regards it as beyond dispute that God's infinite power "cannot be said to extend to the working of anything which implies a *contradiction:* as that a thing should be and not be at the same time; that the same thing should be made and not be made, or have been and not have been; that twice two should not make four, or that that which is necessarily false should be true." Clarke's acceptance of the scholastic point that God's omnipotence does not extend to contradictions is based on the same reason given by Aquinas: since a contradiction is nothing at all, the putative power to do nothing turns out to be no power at all.

Clarke then notes a second restriction on God's infinite power: "Infinite power cannot be said to extend to those things which imply *natural* imperfection in the being to whom such power is ascribed." He regards it as absurd, for example, to think that a being of infinite power could use that power to weaken itself or destroy itself. Weakness or self-destruction are universally recognized to be inconsistent with the necessary and self-existent being of God. Clarke then makes the move that lays the foundation for his answer to the question, Can God sin? Moral imperfection is a species of natural imperfection. Once it is agreed that an omnipotent God cannot do anything that implies any natural imperfection in His own being, it follows that God cannot do anything that entails moral imperfection. Because infinite knowledge, infinite power, and infinite goodness are perfectly conjoined in the being of God, Clarke argues,

> free choice in a being of infinite knowledge, power and goodness can no more choose to act contrary to these imperfections than knowledge can be ignorance, power be weakness, or goodness malice. So that free choice in such a being may be as certain and steady a principle of action as the necessity of fate. We may therefore as certainly and infallibly rely upon the moral, as upon the natural attributes of God—it being as absolutely impossible for him to act contrary to the one as to divest himself of the other; and as much a contradiction to suppose him choosing to do anything inconsistent with his justice, goodness and truth as to suppose him divested of infinity, power or existence.
>
> From hence it follows, that though God is both perfectly free and also infinitely powerful, yet he cannot possibly do anything that is evil. The reason of this is also evident. Because, as it is manifest infinite power cannot extend to natural contradictions which imply a destruction of that very power by which they must be supposed to be effected, so neither can

[10]Samuel Clarke, A *Discourse Concerning the Being and Attributes of God* (London: John and Paul Knapton, 1738), Proposition 10.

it extend to moral contradictions which imply a destruction of some other attributes as necessarily belonging to the divine nature as power. I have already shown that justice, goodness and truth are necessarily in God, even as necessarily as power and understanding, and knowledge of the nature of things. It is, therefore, as impossible and contradictory to suppose his will should choose to do anything contrary to justice, goodness or truth as that his power should be able to do anything inconsistent with power. It is no diminution of power not to be able to do things which are no object of power. And it is in like manner no diminution either of power or liberty to have such a perfect and unalterable rectitude of will as never possibly to choose to do anything inconsistent with that rectitude.[11]

Clarke's point seems to be this: creative power and moral strength are distinguishable in God's creatures. If we suppose an omnipotent being (possessing total creative power) who lacks moral perfection, such a being would indeed lack something if it could not sin. But in God's case, the inability to sin does not constitute an imperfection. Rather, it would be an imperfection if God could sin. The reason God cannot sin is because He is omnipotent and because His omnipotence is necessarily conjoined with moral perfection. If God did sin, it would prove His impotence. God is capable of doing everything that is logically possible and consistent with His perfect will. As Jerome Gellman puts it, "If God is omnipotent, then He can bring about any state of affairs logically possible for an essentially perfect being to bring about."[12] "To be powerless with respect to perversity [that is, powerless to avoid perversity] is to be *imperfect*, but to be unable to lie is a perfection."[13] The power to sin is the power to fall short of perfection. Since this is the opposite of omnipotence, God's inability to sin is not inconsistent with His omnipotence; rather, it is entailed by His omnipotence.

The compatibility of God's omnipotence and His inability to sin may be viewed as an extension of the claim that the law of non-contradiction is a necessary constraint on divine power. As we saw in chapter 1, the word *God* has descriptive significance. Among other things, it includes perfect goodness. Therefore, while no logical contradiction results from ascribing a certain action like sinning to a human being, the action does become self-contradictory when attributed to God.

> In our civilization, and thus in our language, it would not be strictly proper to call a being "God" whose actions were not perfectly good or whose commands were not the best of moral directives. That God is good

---

[11]Ibid., Proposition 12.

[12]Jerome Gellman, "Omnipotence and Impeccability," *The New Scholasticism* 51 (1977): 36.

[13]Ibid., p. 33.

is a truth of language, and not an ethical contingency, since one of the usual *criteria* of Godhood is that the actions and commands of such a being are perfectly good. . . . "God is good," therefore, is trivially true in the same way as "Saints are good."[14]

No contradiction exists, therefore, between the propositions "God is omnipotent" and "God cannot sin."

OMNIPOTENCE AND THE POWER TO CHANGE THE PAST

Imagine a person who has just learned that a loved one has been involved in a plane crash. The first reports indicate that of the one hundred people on the plane, eighty-five died. It would be natural for any person in that situation to breathe a prayer that her loved one on the plane might have been spared. Since the event in question belongs to the past and the people now dead have been dead for hours, this prayer appears to be a request that God change the past. Does such a prayer make sense?

From one perspective, it does not. Most of us believe that although the future may be open (in the sense that people can take actions that will bring it about), the past is closed and nothing can be done now to alter what has already happened. In other words, most human beings are fatalists with respect to the past.

If this view is true, then praying for the past to be changed is either useless or trivial. Either the event that is prayed for has already happened or it has not. If one is praying that what has already happened should happen, the prayer is redundant. If on the other hand, one prays for the opposite of what has already happened, the prayer is hopeless. At least, it is hopeless if fatalism about the past is justified. But is it?

Medieval theologians wondered whether it makes sense to ask if God's omnipotence extends to changing the past. A negative answer would seem to impose a rather severe restriction on God's power. After all, if the past lies outside the scope of an omnipotent being's power, then a situation that might lie within his power today would be beyond his power tomorrow. The proposition, "God can do X," could be true today but false tomorrow.

The position of Thomas Aquinas on this subject has been widely accepted by Christian theologians. To claim that God can change the past, he believed, asserts a contradiction and thus falls under the more general claim that no omnipotent being can do anything that involves a contradiction.

As was said above . . . there does not fall under the scope of God's omnipotence anything that implies a contradiction. Now that the past should not have been implies a contradiction. For as it implies a contradiction to say that Socrates is sitting, and is not sitting, so does it to say that he sat, and did not sit. But to say that he did sit is to say that it happened in the past. To say that he did not sit, is to say that it did not happen. Whence, that the past should not have been, does not come under the scope of divine power.[15]

If it is a fact that something happened in the past, then any proposition describing that state of affairs (such as "Socrates sat") is true. If it were possible for the past to be changed, then the contradictory proposition "Socrates did not sit" would be true. The suggestion then that the past can be changed appears to imply a logically impossible state of affairs, namely, that both "Socrates sat" and "Socrates did not sit" are true. Extending Aquinas's remarks, E. J. Khamara suggests that changing the past may mean "either bringing it about that what has happened has not happened, or bringing it about that what has not happened has happened; and in either case what is envisaged is a logical impossibility."[16] Khamara concludes that "an omnipotent being can have no power over the past because to have such a power would involve ability to bring about logical necessities or logical impossibilities, and these are already excluded from his domain."[17] Thus it seems clear that if God's changing the past is understood in the sense suggested by Aquinas, a contradiction is implied and the view is false.

Some writers, however, have suggested a different approach to the question. The consideration of God's power over the past should, they think, be viewed as an investigation of whether God can *bring about* the past in the sense that his causal activity can be directed toward the past. It seems obvious that human beings can bring about the *future*. That is, their causal activity can be directed toward the future and can bring about future effects. I have it in my power, for example, to bring it about that at five o'clock today, I comb my hair. Is it possible that God's causal activity can be directed toward the *past* so as to bring about a past effect? Understood in this way, the contemplated activity (bringing about the past) does not appear to be logically impossible.[18]

But even if the claim that bringing about the past is logically possible, it remains to be seen whether the notion makes any sense. Any past event is part of a linked series of other events. Consequently, if one believes that it makes sense to think of God changing an event in the

---

[15]Aquinas, *Summa Theologica* I, 25, 4, p. 139.

[16]E. J. Khamara, "In Defense of Omnipotence," *Philosophical Quarterly* 28 (1978): 222.

[17]Ibid., p. 223.

[18]The claim that bringing about the past is not logically impossible has been argued by Michael Dummett in his article, "On Bringing About the Past," *Philosophical Review* 73 (1964): 338–59.

past, events subsequent to the one changed by God would also have to be changed. To help us picture or conceptualize what this might mean, imagine watching a film. The film stops and then rewinds with everything in reverse until the event that is to be changed is reached. The film, let us say, is of someone kicking a soccer ball. At first we see the soccer ball lying still on the grass. Suddenly a swinging foot comes into view; the foot makes contact with the ball and, following the impact, the ball sails into the air and finally descends far down the field, bouncing for a while until it comes to rest in the grass. But now suppose the film is stopped at this point and run backwards. What do we see? The ball is once again lying motionless in the grass. Then, for no reason, without any apparent cause, it begins rolling and then bounding and then soaring through the air until we see it contact a retreating foot. Upon touching the foot, the ball is absolutely motionless. We might imagine another film run backwards in which autumn leaves lying on the ground slowly begin to drift upwards and attach to the branches of a tree. As more and more leaves rise upwards, the leaves begin to change color from red, brown, and gold to a bright green. Soon the leaves begin to curl up into buds which finally disappear into the branches. To anyone unaware that he is watching a film in reverse, such visions could be rather unsettling. These examples simply raise the question whether we can at all conceptualize what it is to bring about the past.

Three arguments support the contention that no sense can be made of the claim that an omnipotent being or anyone else can bring about the past.[19]

1. The view that it is possible to bring about the past eliminates the difference between cause and effect. As David Hume noted, reasoning about cause and effect is fundamental to all reasoning about matters of fact, about significant and informative propositions about the world. Whatever else we mean by saying that x causes y, we certainly mean that x comes before y. The notion of a cause coming after its effect would certainly upset our normal categories of thinking. If soccer balls could suddenly begin moving by themselves in the fashion of our rewinding film, we would have serious difficulties relating to the world. We can understand why the ball moves when the player kicks it. But what makes it move when no one hits it? With our notion of cause so affected, we could not make sense out of the world.

2. The view under consideration would obliterate the difference between earlier and later. The word *later* could just as easily be applied

---

[19]The three arguments that follow are adapted from the discussion in Anthony Kenny's *The God of the Philosophers*, pp. 107-8. Kenny's short discussion is not exactly a model of clarity but my discussion follows what he seems to say.

to something that has already happened, as opposed to something that is still future.

3. The theory would also destroy the difference between past and future. There would no longer be any reason to think of the past as closed in some sense. According to this view, it would be just as possible for the past to be open as it is for the future to be open. These three arguments appear to show that the attempt to say that God can bring about the past reduces to absurdity. While there may be many things that we do not know, we certainly know the difference between cause and effect, between earlier and later, and between the past and future. Thus, any view that implies the impossibility of such knowledge is absurd.

Up to this point we have found no serious challenge to the coherence of the attribute of omnipotence. Answers found in the writings of medieval thinkers still hold up amazingly well. The things that God apparently cannot do can be explained either as things that are logically impossible or as things that result from defective power. None of the problems supports the conclusion that omnipotence is an incoherent notion or that the *real* power of God is limited in some way. However, some people have thought that another kind of problem expressed in certain paradoxes of omnipotence cannot be covered by the scholastic arguments.

THE PARADOX OF OMNIPOTENCE

Philosophers and theologians who grant that God cannot do the logically impossible point out that there are other actions attributable to God that threaten the coherence of the concept of omnipotence. Even if one grants that Aquinas was right when he said that God cannot do the logically impossible, that answer does not seem applicable to the problems that arise when we ask if God can create a stone too heavy for God to lift. The action of creating a stone too heavy to lift does not appear self-contradictory in the same way as drawing a square circle is self-contradictory. Questions about God's ability to perform actions like creating a stone too heavy for Him to lift pose the theist with a dilemma. If God can create the stone too heavy for God to lift, there is something God cannot do (namely, lift the stone). And if God cannot create the stone too heavy for Him to lift, there is still something He cannot do (in this case, create the stone). Either God can or cannot create such a stone. Therefore, in either case, there is something God cannot do; and in either case, we seem forced to conclude that God is not omnipotent.

In a widely discussed analysis of the paradox, George Mavrodes argues that Aquinas's original point about logical possibility can be applied to the new puzzle of the stone.[20] Mavrodes points out that in order for the critic's conclusion to follow, one must first assume that God is omnipotent. After all, if God is not omnipotent, there is no puzzle since the phrase "a stone too heavy for God to lift" would in all likelihood not be self-contradictory. If the argument begins by assuming that God is not omnipotent, the conclusion ("God is not omnipotent") would only repeat the beginning assumption, thus making the entire argument trivial. Thus the paradox of omnipotence must begin by presupposing that God is omnipotent. Once the assumption is made, however, Aquinas's argument becomes relevant. Once one grants that "God is omnipotent" is necessarily true, it follows that "God cannot create a stone too heavy for God to lift" becomes a contradiction. Mavrodes concludes that the paradoxes of omnipotence fail "because they propose, as tests of God's power, putative tasks whose descriptions are self-contradictory. Such pseudo-tasks, not falling within the realm of possibility, are not objects of power at all. Hence the fact that they cannot be performed implies no limit on the power of God, and hence no defect in the doctrine of omnipotence."[21]

In a subsequent article, Harry Frankfurt sought to defuse a possible objection to Mavrodes from any critic who, like Descartes, should reject the law of noncontradiction as a delimitation of the power of God. As Frankfurt notes, even if the Cartesian is correct and the law of non-contradiction does not define the limits of God's power, nothing very significant follows. In fact, we only have a new way of resolving the paradox of omnipotence.

> Suppose, then, that God's omnipotence enables Him to do even what is logically impossible and that He actually creates a stone too heavy for Him to lift. The critic plays into his hands. . . . For why should God not be able to perform the task in question? To be sure, it is a task—the task of lifting a stone which he cannot lift—whose description is self-contradictory. But if God is supposed capable of performing one task whose description is self-contradictory—that of creating the problematic stone in the first place—why should He not be supposed capable of performing another—that of lifting the stone? After all, is there any greater trick in performing two logically impossible tasks than there is in performing one?
>
> If an omnipotent being can do what is logically impossible, then he cannot only create situations which he cannot handle but also, since he is

---

[20]George Mavrodes, "Some Puzzles Concerning Omnipotence," *The Philosophical Review* 72 (1963): 221–23.
[21]Ibid., p. 223.

not bound by the limits of consistency, he can handle situations which he cannot handle.[22]

Suppose a theologian concludes, however, that the question, "Can God create a stone too heavy for God to lift?" must be answered in the negative.[23] Suppose this theologian figures something in the doctrine of omnipotence must be given up but wants to surrender as little as possible. Could God's infinite power with regard to lifting be retained, while limiting only slightly God's power with respect to creating? Following an example developed by C. Wade Savage, we might imagine one being (y) who cannot lift a stone heavier than seventy pounds. If some other being (x) cannot create a stone heavier than y can lift, then obviously x's power to create is limited. But suppose that y can lift a stone of any weight; in other words, imagine that y's lifting power is unlimited. Then it follows that if x cannot create a stone too heavy for y to lift, x's power to create is not limited at all. What then has our theologian surrendered?

> Is it the unlimited power of God to create stones? No doubt. But what stone is it which God is now precluded from creating? The stone too heavy for Him to lift, of course. But . . . nothing in the argument required the theologian to admit any limit on God's power with regard to the lifting of stones. He still holds that to be unlimited. And if God's power to lift is infinite, then His power to create may run to infinity also without outstripping the first power. The supposed limitation turns out to be no limitation at all, since it is specified only by reference to another power which is itself infinite. Our theologian need have no regrets, for he has given up nothing. The doctrine of the power of God remains just what it was before.[24]

It seems clear then that the so-called paradoxes of omnipotence can be handled in the same general terms as Aquinas's dictum that omnipotence does not extend to things that are logically impossible.

CONCLUSION

Enough has been said to permit an answer to two questions: How should "omnipotence" be defined? and Is the concept of omnipotence logically coherent?

William Rowe seems to have included the necessary qualifications

---

[22]Harry G. Frankfurt, "The Logic of Omnipotence," *The Philosophical Review* 74 (1964): 263.

[23]The discussion in this paragraph follows C. Wade Savage's "The Paradox of the Stone," *The Philosophical Review* 76 (1967): 74–79. Savage borrows the key point of his argument from the Mavrodes article already cited.

[24]Mavrodes, "Some Puzzles Concerning Omnipotence," p. 223.

when he defines "omnipotence" to mean that "God can do anything that is an absolute possibility (i.e., is logically possible) *and not inconsistent with any of his basic attributes.*"[25] Among other things, Rowe's definition would rule out any problem about the possibility of God's sinning. Since "doing evil is inconsistent with being perfectly good, and since being perfectly good is a basic attribute of God, the fact that God cannot do evil will not conflict with the fact that he is omnipotent."[26] If Aquinas was correct that changing the past is logically impossible, Rowe's definition would also apply in that case. Kenny goes just a bit further in his definition:

> Divine omnipotence, therefore, if it is to be a coherent notion, must be something less than the complete omnipotence which is the possession of all logically possible powers. It must be a narrower omnipotence, consisting in the possession of all logically possible powers which it is logically possible for a being with the attributes of God to possess.[27]

Is the concept of omnipotence coherent? It would seem so. Even J. L. Mackie, whose opposition to theism is easily documented, acknowledges: "Once we have decided that omnipotence is not to include the power to achieve logical impossibilities—and it must not include this, if it is to be discussable—there cannot be any contradiction within the concept itself."[28] I conclude then that the concept of omnipotence is coherent. No contradiction is involved in affirming that God is essentially omnipotent.

---

[25]William Rowe, *Philosophy of Religion* (Encino, Calif.: Dickenson, 1978), p. 9.
[26]Ibid.
[27]Kenny, *The God of the Philosophers*, p. 98.
[28]Mackie, "Omnipotence," pp. 24–25.

Chapter 4

Divine Omniscience and Human Freedom

Divine omniscience means that God holds no false beliefs. Not only are all of God's beliefs true, the range of his knowledge is total; He knows all true propositions. Is this divine omniscience incompatible with belief in human free will? This is one of the major challenges the theist must face. The problem arises from what it means to know anything in general and what it would mean to know the future in particular.

When any person knows something (a proposition), at least two conditions must be present. First, the person must believe the proposition in question; and second, the believed proposition must be true.[1] If Jennifer knows that today is Jeff's birthday, then Jennifer believes that today is Jeff's birthday. Believing a proposition is a necessary condition for knowing it. If Jennifer doesn't believe that today is Jeff's birthday, she cannot know it. Thus knowing p (any proposition) implies believing p. But just as clearly, Jennifer cannot have knowledge of some proposition unless that proposition is true. If Jennifer "knows" p, and p is false, then Jennifer's claim to knowledge is mistaken. She may think that she knows today is Jeff's birthday but she is wrong. She does not have knowledge.

If the body of true propositions known by an omniscient being includes all true propositions about what human beings will do in the future, a serious consequence for human freedom arises. Obviously, it

---

[1]While knowledge includes more than true belief, it cannot mean less. Identifying the other component(s) of knowledge has proven extremely difficult, and philosophers disagree strongly among themselves. Plato's dialogue *Theaetetus* is helpful to read in this regard. Plato agreed that knowledge is true belief plus something else. But exactly what this something else is is difficult to say. Most of the theories that have been proposed are discussed in the first edition of Roderick Chisholm's *Theory of Knowledge* (Englewood Cliffs, N.J.: Prentice-Hall, 1966), chap. 1.

51

is impossible for any omniscient being to hold even one false belief. Since God foreknows what Jeff will do at 8 P.M. tomorrow, it appears as though Jeff *must* do what God foreknows he will do. But if Jeff *must* do whatever God knows he will do, in what sense is Jeff's action free? If God foreknows what Jeff will do in the future, does Jeff have the ability not to do what God foreknows? It seems highly unlikely. If Jeff had *that* power (the power to do something other than what God foreknows), then God could have been mistaken. God would have held a false belief in which case God's foreknowledge would have actually been fore-ignorance. But this is clearly impossible. If God has true foreknowledge of what human beings will do in the future, it seems that those actions are determined. But if those actions are not determined and human beings really do have the power either to do something or not, then it seems to follow that God lacks omniscience. The literature on this question is extensive.[2] This chapter will investigate the most frequently suggested answers to the problem.

THE REINTERPRETATION OF GOD'S RELATIONSHIP TO TIME

In the long history of Christian thought, the theory most frequently used to reconcile divine foreknowledge and human freedom involves interpreting God's eternal existence as timelessness. This view appears in the writings of such thinkers as Augustine, Boethius, Anselm, and Aquinas.

The analogy between God's vision of *future* human actions and a human being's *present* perception is crucial to this argument. When Mr. Brown sees Mr. Smith scratching his ear, Brown's perception of what Smith does obviously cannot have any causal influence on Smith's action. What any person perceives in the present is simple vision, a vision that cannot cause or make necessary that which is being perceived. Similarly, whatever God might perceive in the present would likewise lack any necessitating or causal effect on what He perceives. But because God is outside of time, is timeless, all of God's knowledge occurs in *His* eternal present. There is no future for God; there is no past for God. Everything that belongs to the human past and everything that will happen in the human future is, on this view of God, eternally present to God's consciousness. Technically, then, God does not have *fore*knowledge even though He infallibly knows everything that will happen in the future. But since His knowledge of the

---

[2]A partial listing of some of the more important sources can be found in the bibliography of Anthony Kenny's book, *The God of the Philosophers* (Oxford: Clarendon, 1979).

human future exists in His present, His knowledge does not cause or necessitate the future. According to Boethius,

> If human and divine present may be compared, just as you see certain things in this your present time, so God sees all things in His eternal present. So that this divine foreknowledge does not change the nature and property of things; it simply sees things present to it exactly as they will happen at some time as future events. It makes no confused judgements of things, but with one glance of its mind distinguishes all that is to come to pass whether it is necessitated or not. Similarly you, when you see at the same time a man walking on the earth and the sun rising in the sky, although the two sights coincide yet you distinguish between them and judge the one to be willed and the other necessitated. In the same way the divine gaze looks down on all things without disturbing their nature; to Him they are present things, but under the condition of time they are future things. And so it comes about that when God knows that something is going to occur and knows that no necessity to be is imposed upon it, it is not opinion, but rather knowledge founded upon truth.[3]

Since divine timelessness is the subject of chapter 6 (where it is given more complete consideration), the problems generated by the doctrine are best left till then. For now, two observations: (1) The doctrine's utility in providing a convenient solution to the apparent conflict between divine omniscience and human freedom is one of the strongest reasons for its acceptance. (2) But utility alone is not a test of truth and the theory will have to be defended against several rather weighty objections. How, for example, is it possible for a timeless being, a being who is totally removed from time, to act within time? The Judeo-Christian doctrines of creation and providence certainly imply a God who acts within time.

THE REINTERPRETATION OF HUMAN FREEDOM

Many thinkers have decided that if divine omniscience and human freedom are incompatible, any compromise will have to take place on the side of freedom. This has usually been effected by redefining human freedom so as to make it compatible with determinism. In the struggle between determinism and indeterminism, philosophers divide into compatibilists and incompatibilists. A compatibilist believes that freedom and determinism can be reconciled in some way; an incompatibilist believes that they cannot. Major Christian thinkers like Augustine, Luther, Calvin, and Jonathan Edwards did not actually repudiate human freedom. They redefined the notion of human freedom so that it is compatible with determinism.

---

[3]Boethius, *The Consolation of Philosophy*, trans. V. E. Watts (London: Penguin, 1969), Book 5, chap. 6, pp. 165–66.

Human beings may be said to be free in two quite different senses. The *liberty of indifference* explains human freedom as the ability either to do something or not. Understood in this sense, Jones's decision to watch the T.V. news on channel four rather than on channel five is free if and only if it is completely indifferent (undetermined) which channel he turns to. In order to be genuinely free in the sense of indifference, a person must have the ability either to do something or not. The *liberty of spontaneity*, on the other hand, explains human freedom as the ability to do whatever the person wants to do. On this second view, the question of the person's ability to do otherwise is irrelevant; the key question is whether he is able to do.what he most wants to do.

The liberty of indifference is an incompatibilist definition of freedom, while the liberty of spontaneity is a form of compatibilism. If liberty is understood in terms of indifference, Jones's decision is free if and only if he is either free to watch channel four or not to watch channel four. But if liberty is understood in terms of spontaneity, Jones can still be free even if his decision to watch channel four is determined. Jones may have been hypnotized previously and told to watch only one station; or his set may be broken so it receives only one station; or someone holding a gun might threaten his life if he turns to any channel other than four. But it is obvious that whatever antecedent events might cause Jones to watch channel four, it is possible that it is also the channel that he most wants to watch. As long as his act is an expression of what he wants, then his action is free even if his wants are themselves determined.

If human freedom can be adequately explained in terms of the liberty of spontaneity, then there would seem to be no problem reconciling divine foreknowledge and human freedom. Men and women would remain free even if their decisions and their wants were determined in some sense. God would simply see to it that His creatures want to do what He has determined them to do.

Martin Luther accepted this compatibilist approach to human freedom. As Anthony Kenny explains Luther's position: "The human will is like a beast of burden: if God rides it it wills and goes where God wills; if Satan rides it it wills and goes where Satan wills. It must go where its rider bids, and it is not free to choose its rider."[4] For Luther (according to Kenny), "both good men and bad men do what they want: what they lack is the ability to change their desires." The human will "is not free in the sense that it cannot change itself from a bad will into a good one; it can only passively undergo such a change at the hand of God."[5]

---

[4]Kenny, *The God of the Philosophers*, p. 73.
[5]Ibid.

A proper evaluation of theological compatibilism would require too lengthy a detour in this study. Critics of the theory frequently resort to an analogy of a man imprisoned in a locked room. As long as the prisoner wants to remain in the locked room, he is free—at least this is the claim of those who defend the liberty of spontaneity. But to claim that the imprisoned man is free, stretches the meaning of "freedom" far beyond the bounds of ordinary usage. Compatibilists, in turn, counter with the claim that this argument (concerning the stretched meaning of "freedom") begs the question.

The most serious attack against theological compatibilism maintains that the position entails that God is ultimately responsible for the evil in the world. The issues raised by this objection are topics of perennial debate in the history of philosophy, and exceed the capacity of this brief introduction to the concept of God. The problem is well and fully discussed elsewhere.[6] We will leave what might be called "the compatibilist gambit" with the observation that its eventual success will require its advocate to explain how it is that God is not responsible for the moral evil in the world.

DO PROPOSITIONS ABOUT THE FUTURE HAVE TRUTH-VALUE?

Another proposed solution to problems raised by divine omniscience in relation to human freedom concerns the truth-value of statements about the future. Corresponding to every possible state of affairs in the future is a proposition. For example, corresponding to the possible state of affairs, Ted Kennedy's running for the presidency in 1988, is the proposition "Ted Kennedy will run for the presidency in 1988." Clearly, the proposition "Ted Kennedy *ran* for the presidency in 1980" is true. But many philosophers have expressed doubt that propositions about future contingent events have any truth-value at all; that is, they have suggested that propositions about the future ("Ted Kennedy will run for the presidency in 1988") are neither true nor false.

One source for this theory is chapter nine of Aristotle's *De Interpretatione*. According to Aristotle, any proposition about that which

---

[6]The writing on this subject is extensive. For one who maintains the inability of Calvinist thinkers to absolve God of moral responsibility for the world's evil, see Kenny, *The God of the Philosophers*, pp. 86–87. For a Calvinist counter-argument, consult Gordon H. Clark, *Religion, Reason and Revelation* (Philadelphia: Presbyterian and Reformed Publishing Co., 1961), pp. 204ff. Clark thinks that all talk about holding God accountable or responsible for what He does is incoherent. If God is the sovereign Lord of the universe, there is no one or nothing to which He is accountable besides Himself. Alvin Plantinga, a Reformed thinker, advocates an approach to the problem of evil based on the liberty of indifference. See his *God, Freedom and Evil* (New York: Harper and Row, 1974).

has already happened must be either true or false. But is it the case, he asked, that propositions about the future must be either true or false? Take, for example, the proposition "There will be a sea fight tomorrow." If this proposition about the future already has a truth value (that is, if it is either true or false *today*), then it seems to follow that the future is fixed. If the proposition "There will be a sea fight tomorrow" were true *today*, then it would be impossible for there not to be a sea fight tomorrow. For if the sea fight did not occur, then our proposition could not have been true. But since it is true, the sea fight is inevitable.

Most interpreters read Aristotle's argument as a *reductio ad absurdum*. As Kenny explains: "If future-tensed propositions about singulars are already true, then fatalism follows: but fatalism is absurd; therefore, since many future events are not yet determined, statements about such events are not yet true or false, though they later will be."[7] The relevance of Aristotle's position for resolving the omniscience-human freedom problem should be obvious. If propositions about future, free human actions have no truth-value, then they cannot possibly be known by anyone including an omniscient God. God's inability to know the future should not count against His omniscience, since the power to know is constrained only in cases where there is something to know. But if no propositions about future, free actions can be true, they cannot be the object of knowledge for anyone, including God.

This view severely limits the knowledge of God—a major difficulty—and apparently is incompatible with the Bible's account of God's ability to predict the future.[8] If propositions about the future are neither true nor false, it is logically impossible for God to predict the future.[9] The belief that God does predict the future presumes that God knows what He is talking about. But since God does not know what cannot be known, it follows that God cannot predict the future. The most God might be able to do on Aristotle's view is make a good guess, an epistemological liability when compared to the classical view. The denial of truth-values to propositions about future contingents has not received a sympathetic hearing from many traditional Christians. It is an extreme position that is difficult to reconcile with much that Scripture and orthodox theology affirm about God's knowledge of the future.

---

[7]Kenny, *The God of the Philosophers*, p. 52.

[8]I am presuming that any view wishing to be considered under the label of *Christian* theism has at least a prima facie obligation to pass what might be called the Scripture-Dogma test. If it fails this test, its credibility as a *Christian* doctrine comes into question and must be established on other grounds, if possible.

[9]The sense of "predict" here is to foretell with absolute certainty what will happen.

"THE BOOK OF THE FUTURE"

One model that might be useful in suggesting solutions to the puzzle of divine omniscience and human freedom involves imagining the existence of a document we might call the "book of the future." Before this imaginary book is opened, it is possible to conceive three different scenarios. According to the first of these, when God opens the book, He finds written there every true proposition about the future. This represents the theory that God knows everything that will happen in the future.[10]

According to a second possible scenario, God opens the book of the future only to find that every page is blank. This pictures the Aristotelian theory that propositions about the future have no truth-value. Since, on that view, there are no true propositions about the future, the pages in any book about the future would have to be blank. Knowledge about the future is impossible for any being including God. This apparent limitation of omniscience is not viewed with alarm by its adherents since the doctrine of omniscience requires only that God know everything that can be known. The mere fact that God cannot know something that cannot be known by any being would not compromise His omniscience. The Aristotelian view, however, does suffer from other problems, already noted.

According to a third scenario, the book is incomplete. That is, some pages contain propositions, but there are gaps, sometimes very large gaps. Many pages may be completely blank. This scenario suggests that God possesses only partial knowledge about the future because He freely chooses to restrict His knowledge of the future in order to preserve some measure of human freedom. This picture would be compatible with a somewhat different theory according to which God has unerring knowledge of some specific future events, namely, those which He has decreed must happen. But of future events that are not the subject of divine decree, God's knowledge is impossible.

Robert H. Ayers thinks that the views suggested by this third scenario should be understood as arguments for a limitation of divine omniscience along the lines of Aquinas's limitation of omnipotence.

If the meaning of God's omnipotence is preserved by saying that God can

---

[10]Of course, the analogy is also misleading in some important theological respects. It is faulty because it suggests that God can come to know the future, i.e., that the future is something that God might fail to know at a certain time. It also misleads by suggesting that God's knowledge is mediated by something else, in this case, by our "book." But if these factors are bracketed and viewed as extraneous and irrelevant to our basic point, the model can still serve its purpose.

do everything that is logically possible to do, why can't the meaning of God's omniscience be preserved by saying that God can know everything it is logically possible to know? That is, God can know all past and present actualities and all future possibilities. Surely, if omniscience means to know, at any given moment, all that there is to know and if time is not an illusion, then to know future contingents as indetermined and future, relative to some past and determined actuality, is an acceptable meaning of the term "omniscience."[11]

In terms of my model of the book of the future, God freely chooses to limit His own knowledge of the future by refusing to peek between the covers of the book of the future. A similar view has been advanced by John Lucas:

The real solution to the problem of God's omniscience is to be found by drawing a parallel with his omnipotence. Although God is able to do all things, we do not think he does do all things. . . . We allow that some things happen against God's will. . . . If God is prepared to compromise his omnipotence for the sake of human freedom, surely then he would be prepared to compromise his omniscience also. If he suffers his will to be confined in order that his creatures may have room to make their own decisions, he must allow his understanding to be abridged in order to allow men privacy to form their own plans for themselves. It seems to me entirely unobjectionable that God should limit his infallible knowledge as he does his power, in order to let us be independent of him.[12]

If this theory is taken to mean that God chooses not to know *anything* about the future, the view comes into obvious conflict with the biblical data and most traditional thinking about God. It is clearly inconsistent with the belief that God, at the very least, knows *some* future actions, for example, that Judas would betray Jesus. To get around this problem, Richard Swinburne suggests that God might be said to know *some* future actions, such as those that are necessitated by past actions or by God's own decrees. But there would still remain a large number of future actions which God would freely choose not to foreknow. Understood properly, this does not compromise God's omniscience, according to Swinburne. On his view, God

is omniscient if he knows about everything except those future states and their consequences which are not physically necessitated by anything in the past; and if he knows that he does not know about those future states. If there is any future state which is not physically necessitated by goings-on

---

[11]Robert H. Ayers, "A Viable Theodicy for Christian Apologetics," *The Modern Schoolman* 52 (1975), pp. 395–96.

[12]John Lucas, *The Freedom of the Will* (London: Oxford University Press, 1970), p. 75.

in the past or present, then, of logical necessity, no person can know now that it will happen—without the possibility of error.[13]

In other words, God creates a sphere (that of future, free actions) where divine knowledge is excluded. So long as such a restriction is a result of God's free choice, and so long as God knows that He does not have this knowledge, no compromise of the divine omniscience would result. "That God is omniscient only in the attenuated sense would of course . . . have resulted from his own choice. In choosing to preserve his own freedom (and to give others freedom), he limits his own knowledge of what is to come."[14]

The Swinburne-Lucas-Ayer position appears plausible until one begins to ask some innocent-looking questions. Suppose we grant that God does not *know* the future (or at least large parts of the future); can God nonetheless hold *beliefs* about the future? If we follow Swinburne, it might make sense to suppose that God freely chooses not to know many things about the future. But what reason could we possibly have for supposing that God refuses to hold beliefs about the future? If we grant that God does not *know* who will win the World Series, what is wrong with supposing that God can hold *beliefs* about who will win? Is there any difference between the beliefs that God might hold and well-grounded guesses? It is difficult to see how Swinburne could avoid allowing God to make highly intelligent guesses about future contingents. Obviously, God's guesses would be far more reliable than ours since He would still have full and complete knowledge of all past and present circumstances that will have an effect on the future.[15] To adopt the view that God can hold beliefs about the future, however, seems to entail the possibility that some of God's beliefs may turn out to be *false*. But once it becomes possible for any of God's beliefs about the future to be false, what will have happened to the omniscience of God which entails that God holds no false beliefs? Even if Swinburne holds out for the possibility that all God's beliefs about the future were true, he would have to add the proviso that God does not know that all His beliefs about the future are true. Swinburne's way of preserving human freedom while retaining divine foreknowledge produces a supposedly omniscient

---

[13]Swinburne, *The Coherence of Theism* (Oxford: Clarendon, 1977), pp. 175–76.

[14]Ibid., p. 176. For a similar view held by an American Fundamentalist, see T. W. Brents, *The Gospel Plan of Salvation* (Nashville, Tenn.: Gospel Advocate, reprinted 1966), pp. 92–108.

[15]Swinburne: "As regards men, their choices are much influenced by circumstances and this makes it possible for a being who knows all the circumstances to predict human behavior correctly most of the time, but always with the possibility that men may falsify those predictions." *The Coherence of Theism*, p. 176.

being who not only does not know a great many things, but who also possibly holds a great many false beliefs.

Advocates of classical Thomism have not been silent in the face of Swinburne's theorizing. According to one, Swinburne's explication of a weak sense of omniscience is logically incompatible with two pivotal doctrines of classical theism, namely that God is omnipotent and that God is Creator-sustainer of the world. Roland Teske makes the first claim—that omniscience in Swinburne's weak sense is inconsistent with omnipotence—in the following way. First, Swinburne's view of omniscience begins by assuming that the events in the world cause God's knowledge. Specifically, God's knowledge of future contingents would be dependent on, caused by, conditioned by, or changed by the events that happen. But Aquinas and other classical theists have taught that God's knowledge *causes* what happens.

> The basic question about God's knowledge is whether things exist because God knows them or whether God knows them because they exist. Augustine . . . and Aquinas . . . maintain that beings exist because God knows them. Hence, God's knowledge stands in relation to created things as the knowledge of a craftsman stands to his products. As the craftsman's knowledge is the cause of his products, so God's knowledge is the cause of his creatures. [16]

Teske expresses a dominant concern of every theist. Whatever else may be involved in theism, it certainly teaches that the creation depends upon God for its existence.

> If God cannot be the cause of new existents and occurrences and if such new existents and occurrences are at least in some cases contingent, then there are many existents and occurrences which, though not logically impossible, cannot be caused by God. Indeed, if God's knowledge of all existents and occurrences is contingent upon their existence and occurrence and caused by these existents and occurrences, then God cannot cause any existents and occurrences. [17]

Teske's claim that Swinburne's weak sense of omniscience severely restricts and may even abrogate the notion of divine omnipotence must be taken seriously.

In his second objection, Teske argues that the weak sense of omniscience is incompatible with a belief in God as Creator. In speaking of God as Creator of the world, Teske means

> that he is the cause of all existents and occurrences apart from himself— not merely in the sense that he originally made the world *ex nihilo sui et*

---

[16]Roland H. Teske, S.J., "Omniscience, Omnipotence and Divine Transcendence," *The New Scholasticism* 53 (1979): 280.

[17]Ibid., p. 281.

subjecti, but in the sense that he is at present the first cause of all existents and occurrences in this world.[18]

But the weak sense of omniscience implies that new events and beings must exist prior to God's knowledge of them. This entails that God cannot be the cause of such independent existents and occurrences.

> If God's knowledge is conditioned by and dependent upon events that occur in this world, then he cannot have a provident governance of this world. . . . Without the causal priority of God's knowledge over events in this world, it would seem that God could not have produced the world in any sense or that he caused it without knowing what he was doing and then saw what he had done.[19]

Teske expresses legitimate complaints that ought to be concerns of any theist. Such are the problems, then, with the attempt of Ayers, Lucas, and Swinburne to conceive of God as voluntarily restricting the sphere of His omniscience.

Peter Geach is also interested in defending an indeterminate future. But he takes a different tack, comparing God's knowledge of the future to that of a chess master simultaneously playing several games of chess.

> But God is the supreme Grand Master who has everything under his control. Some of the players are consciously helping his plan, others are trying to hinder it; whatever the finite players do, God's plan will be executed; though various lines of God's play will answer to various moves of the finite players. God cannot be surprised or thwarted or cheated or disappointed. God, like some grand master of chess, can carry out his plan even if he has announced it beforehand. "On that square," says the Grand Master, "I will promote my pawn to Queen and deliver checkmate to my adversary": and it is even so. No line of play that finite players may think of can force God to improvise: his knowledge of the game already embraces all the possible variant lines of play, theirs does not.[20]

Unlike Swinburne, Geach wants to preserve some sense of divine omniscience about the future. But he wants to do this without resorting to the timelessness doctrine. Geach suggests that certain propositions about the future are true when they correspond to present tendencies in the world, just as the grand master knows that his opponents tend to make certain moves in certain situations. God has perfect control over the chess board of life. He is able to predict the final mate down to the positions of the pieces on the board; He can even predict the precise

---

[18]Ibid., p. 282.

[19]Ibid., pp. 282–83.

[20]Peter Geach, *Providence and Evil* (Cambridge: Cambridge University Press, 1977), p. 58.

manner of the checkmate. Because God has such control of the game, no move will surprise Him since He knows all the possibilities. In this way, He carries each game through to its predicted conclusion without any possibility of His being surprised, frustrated, disappointed, or defeated. For Geach, God does not simply know the tendencies and intentions of His creatures; even more, He knows the future because He knows His own intentions: "I think God knows the future by *controlling* it. God's knowledge of the future is like man's knowledge of his own intentional actions, not like that of an ideal spectator."[21]

Geach's position bears some resemblance to the view of John Duns Scotus in the late Middle Ages. For Duns Scotus, the ground of God's knowledge of future contingents is God's knowledge of His own will. Geach's theory is an interesting alternative to the other theories we have noted. Unfortunately, the key point in his theory, namely, the precise sense in which God *controls* the actions of free human beings without depriving them of their freedom, never receives the careful analysis it needs. Much of the theory's plausibility seems to result from the interesting analogy of the chess master and Geach's refusal to remove the vagueness found at key points in his picture.

THE APPEAL TO GOD'S SUPPOSED "MIDDLE KNOWLEDGE"

An ingenious but dubious attempt to reconcile divine foreknowledge and human freedom was advanced by the sixteenth-century Jesuit theologian Louis de Molina.[22] Molina began by accepting three claims already noted: (1) future contingent propositions have a truth-value; (2) God knows all true propositions about the future; and (3) human beings are free in the sense of the liberty of indifference, that is, they are free either to do x or not to do x.

One of the easiest ways to get into Molina's system is to use the language of possible worlds that was introduced in the discussion of essential predication in chapter 1. As we saw, there is an infinite number of possible worlds (complete states of affairs), only one of which is the actual or real world. In order for one possible world to differ from another, at least one state of affairs must be different. Let us imagine a possible world in which Judas Iscariot is offered thirty pieces of silver to betray Jesus. We know at least two things about this possible state of affairs: (1) we know that it is also part of the actual world; and (2) we know that the hypothetical proposition "If Judas is offered thirty pieces of silver, then he will betray Jesus," is true.

Now imagine a second possible world that is exactly the same as

---

[21]Ibid., p. 57.
[22]A similar view was held by Francesco Suarez, also a sixteenth-century Jesuit.

the real world with but one difference: in this second possible world, Judas is offered only twenty pieces of silver. This possible state of affairs is referred to by the contrary-to-fact conditional "If Judas had been offered twenty pieces of silver, he would have betrayed Jesus." Is this second hypothetical statement true or false? Since we cannot say for sure, we can only guess. One way to view this second hypothetical situation is to imagine two more possible worlds. In one of them, Judas is offered twenty pieces of silver and betrays Jesus; in the other, Judas is offered the same amount and refuses to betray Jesus.

It is doubtful that any human being could ever know which of these two possible worlds would have become actual if, in fact, Judas had been offered only twenty pieces of silver. But it is basic to Molina's theory that God knows the content of every possible world. God knows what Judas would have done if he had been offered twenty pieces of silver or only one or none at all. In fact, God knows what Judas would have *freely* done in every possible world.

Molina called this strange kind of knowledge "middle knowledge" because it supposedly comes between two other kinds of knowledge that God can have. R. Garrigou-Lagrange explains:

> This knowledge is called middle by reason of its proper object, which is the conditional future or the conditionally free act of the future. It is intermediate between the purely possible which is the object of God's knowledge of simple intelligence, and the contingent future which is the object of God's knowledge of vision. By this middle knowledge, according to Molina, God knows, previous to any predetermining decree, how a free will would act if placed in certain circumstances, and how in certain other cases it would decide otherwise. After that God decides, according to His benevolent designs, to render this free will effective by placing it in those circumstances more or less favorable or unfavorable to it.[23]

In other words, by means of His *natural knowledge*, God knows everything that can be; by means of His *simple vision*, God knows what will be, that is, what will actually occur in the real world; and by means of His *middle knowledge*, God knows what would be if the world were different in some way. Anton Pegis describes God's middle knowledge as "an eternal dress rehearsal in the divine knowledge of all the ways in which man would act under all the circumstances which God would create."[24]

By means of His middle knowledge, then, God knows all possible worlds and what each possible individual would do in them. God then

[23]R. Garrigou-Lagrange, O.P., *God: His Existence and His Nature*, vol. 2 (St. Louis: B. Herder, 1936), p. 82.

[24]Anton Pegis, "Molina and Human Liberty," in *Jesuit Thinkers of the Renaissance*, ed. Gerard Smith, S.J. (Milwaukee: Marquette University Press, 1939), p. 121.

decrees certain antecedent conditions with full knowledge of how the agent will act in that situation. But God's decree does not violate the freedom of the agent. In the case of Judas, God knows that if Judas is offered thirty pieces of silver, Judas will of his own free will choose to betray Jesus. God simply actualizes the set of circumstances in which His will is accomplished. But God's decree in no way interferes with the free choice of His creatures.

Roman Catholic theology quickly decided that Molina's attempt to preserve free will was heretical. It is not difficult to find Catholic objections to Molina. Garrigou-Lagrange writes:

> To this [Molina's theory of middle knowledge] the Thomists have always replied that the middle knowledge conceived to safeguard the freedom of the human will, virtually implies the denial of it. How can God see in a cause [he means here the human will], which by its nature is undetermined as to whether it will act or not, that it will *de facto* act? The supracomprehensive knowledge of a cause cannot enable anyone to see in it a determination which is not there.[25]

In other words, the human will is the relevant cause and if the will is undetermined, there is nothing for God to see via His middle knowledge.

Molina's views have received a revival of sorts at the hands of the Calvinist philosopher, Alvin Plantinga.* In a recent article, R. M. Adams has specifically addressed the presence of Molinistic tendencies within Plantinga's system.[26] Adams expresses doubts about the possibility of middle knowledge, even for God. His basic reason for this skepticism appears to be his inability to see what serves as a ground for contrary-to-fact conditionals. But it is not at all clear why conditionals like "If Saul had never encountered Jesus on the road to Damascus, he would never have become a Christian" need any kind of ground. What prevents such conditionals from just being true? Moreover, Adams's own position is equivocal. He never makes clear whether he thinks

---

[25]Garrigou-Lagrange, *God: His Existence*, pp. 82–83.

*Plantinga is not a Molinist. It has been difficult for some to understand the presence of Molinistic elements in (Calvinist) Plantinga's views, since Molina's position (especially his stress on the liberty of indifference) has been so serviceable to the Arminian system of theology. It is Plantinga's use of the language of possible worlds that results in resemblances between his views and those of Molina. Plantinga thinks he can state his positions in a way, however, that avoids any dependence on middle knowledge. He has received a great deal of attention for his use of the semantics of possible worlds in his discussions of the problem of evil and the ontological argument for the existence of God. See his *God, Freedom and Evil*.

[26]Robert Merrihew Adams, "Middle Knowledge and the Problem of Evil," *American Philosophical Quarterly* 14 (1977): 109–17. None of Adams's points score very heavily against Plantinga.

counterfactual sentences fail to express any proposition at all or whether they simply express propositions that are false.

Even if the objections to the doctrine of middle knowledge leave the question of its truth unclear, the Molinist attempt to reconcile divine foreknowledge and human freedom still has difficulty gaining converts. In a sense, the difficulty of evaluating Molina's theory resembles the earlier problem of appraising the position of Geach. In both cases, a suggestive picture or model was offered: in Geach's case, that of an unbeatable chess master; in Molina's theory, that of an all-knowing God who has the power to "see" not only what will happen in the future but also what would have happened had different circumstances obtained. The pictures that Geach and Molina present make it possible to understand how God might know the future without also determining what human beings do in the future. At least the pictures lead us to *think* we understand. But in both cases, the picture that is offered is not accompanied with the analysis of key concepts that will convert the picture into both an explanation and an argument. This may explain why so many turn away from Molinism and look elsewhere for a satisfactory resolution to the problem of foreknowledge and human freedom.

CONCLUSION

My discussion of the most common solutions to the apparent conflict between divine omniscience and human freedom has not produced a clear winner among the candidates. But perhaps there is a simpler way of resolving the problem. Is it possible that we erred at the beginning by allowing one or two points to slip by too quickly? Perhaps we should take one more look to see if there truly is reason to believe that divine omniscience and human freedom are incompatible.

Perhaps the philosophers of the Middle Ages are a step or two ahead of us. Consider the following statement from Aquinas's *Summa Theologica*:

> Hence also this proposition, *Everything known by God must necessarily be*, is usually distinguished, for it may refer to the thing or to the saying. If it refers to the thing, it is divided and false; for the sense is, *Everything which God knows is necessary*. If understood of the saying, it is composite and true, for the sense is, *This proposition, "That which is known of God is" is necessary.* [27]

Aquinas is saying first of all that the claim "Everything known by God must necessarily be" is a key premise in any argument used to support the alleged incompatibility of omniscience and human freedom. But

---

[27]*Summa Theologica* I, 14, 13, p. 84.

the sentence is ambiguous. It can be understood in two quite different senses. In the *second* sense offered by Aquinas ("this proposition, 'that which is known of God is' is necessary"), it might mean that the proposition "Whatever God knows is true" is a necessary truth. Given that God is essentially omniscient, this second version of the proposition is most assuredly true. But from this claim, absolutely nothing that might detract from the freedom of future human acts follows. While the proposition is true, it does not support any argument that restricts the freedom of future human acts.

Things are quite different, however, with the *first* interpretation which can be read: "Whatever God knows is a necessary truth." This first interpretation of the key premise entails that future human actions are necessary. But the premise of this first interpretation—that everything known by God is a necessary truth—now turns out to be false. Necessary truths, it will be remembered, are statements like those found in mathematics and logic which cannot possibly be false. Statements like "seven plus five equals twelve" do not just happen to be true; they must be true; they are true in all possible worlds. God knows all necessary truths, to be sure. But he also knows a great many truths that are contingent, that are true in some possible worlds but not all. For example, God knows the true proposition, "Abraham Lincoln was assassinated." But obviously this proposition does not express a necessary truth. There are possible worlds in which Lincoln lived to finish out his second term and retired in Cleveland, Ohio. So it turns out that the only relevant interpretation of the key premise in the argument in question is false. [28] Without an argument to show that God's foreknowledge makes all future human acts necessary, there is no need to resort to any of the theories studied in this chapter.

---

[28]Aquinas's strategy is adopted by several contemporary writers who deal with the subject. See Alvin Plantinga, *God, Freedom and Evil*, pp. 66–67, and William Rowe, "Augustine on Foreknowledge and Free Will," *The Review of Metaphysics* 18 (1964): 356–63.

Chapter 5

Omniscience: Two Recent Objections

Two arguments against divine omniscience have received a great deal of attention recently. According to the first of these arguments, divine omniscience is incompatible with the attribute of immutability: it is impossible for a being to be both omniscient and immutable. According to the second, divine omniscience is incompatible with theism itself. That is, if God were omniscient, He could not be the personal God of theism. Omniscience would entail some kind of pantheism in which God would be identical with all human beings. The purpose of this chapter is to explain and evaluate these arguments.

OMNISCIENCE AND IMMUTABILITY

In 1966 Norman Kretzmann provoked much discussion with an article in which he argued that it is logically impossible for a being to be both omniscient and immutable.[1] If God really does know everything, Kretzmann maintained, then He obviously knows many things that undergo change. But if the objects of God's knowledge change, then change must also occur within God. Therefore, it seems, a God who knows everything cannot possibly be a God who is immutable. Though it is possible to argue (as I do in chapter 8) that changes in God's knowledge may pose no threat to a properly formulated doctrine of

---

[1]Norman Kretzmann, "Omniscience and Immutability," *Journal of Philosophy* 63 (1966): 409–21. The major reply to Kretzmann is Hector-Neri Castañeda's article, "Omniscience and Indexical References," *Journal of Philosophy* 64 (1967): 203–10. Though I use different examples, my discussion corresponds to the essential points in the Kretzmann article and to Castañeda's reply. Also worth reading are Anthony Kenny, *God of the Philosophers*, pp. 40ff.; Anthony Kenny, "God and Necessity," in *British Analytical Philosophy*, ed. Bernard Williams and Alan Montefiore (New York: Humanities Press, 1966), especially pp. 146ff.; E. J. Lemmon, "Sentences, Statements and Propositions," also in *British Analytical Philosophy*, pp. 87–108; Swinburne, *The Coherence of Theism*, pp. 164ff.; Paul Helm, "Timelessness and Foreknowledge," *Mind* 84 (1975): 516–27.

divine immutability, yet Kretzmann's position is worth studying because of the interesting questions it raises for divine omniscience.

Consider the following sentences:[2] (1) Christ will be born; (2) Christ is born; and (3) Christ was born. There was a time (when David was king of Israel, let us say) when "Christ will be born" was true. At a later time (4 B.C. or whatever the right year happens to be), the first sentence was false and "Christ is born" became true. Today, "Christ was born" is true and (1) and (2) are false.

Now suppose that God cannot know that the sentence "Christ will be born" was true at one time and is false now. Imagine that at the time God knows "Christ will be born" is true, He cannot for some reason know that "Christ was born" is false. Under such circumstances, it would be difficult to see how we could retain belief in God's omniscience. The doctrine of omniscience clearly commits us to saying that God knows all true propositions; this seems to entail that God also knows when a true sentence ceases to be true. If a sentence like "Christ will be born" is true at one time and false at another, the Christian theist, it appears, must admit that what God knows in this regard changes. As time passes and conditions change, and as the truth-value of many sentences changes, the content of God's knowledge must change. But if all this is so, then a new problem arises: if the content of God's awareness is different from one time to another, then God's awareness changes. In the face of this, how can the theist maintain belief in God's immutability?

Though most people who encounter this problem for the first time sense instinctively that something is fishy, explaining precisely what is wrong can lead into some extremely difficult areas of philosophy. The technical and controversial nature of these issues makes a brief, introductory discussion very difficult. I am going to take a calculated risk and discuss only one strategy for solving the apparent incompatibility of omniscience and immutability.[3] My approach begins with an explanation of a widely held theory about propositions.

Many philosophers distinguish between sentences and propositions. A sentence is some combination of words in a particular language. If a sentence has meaning, its meaning is said to be the proposition expressed by the sentence. Consider, for example, the following sentences: (4) John is the husband of Mary, and (5) Mary is the wife of John. It is clear that (4) and (5) are different sentences that nonetheless

---

[2]The examples are used by Aquinas in *Summa Theologica* I, 14, 15.

[3]A totally different strategy was adopted by Aquinas. See Kenny's discussion of Aquinas's position in *The God of the Philosophers*, pp. 140ff.

refer to the same state of affairs. Both sentences have the same meaning and thus express the same proposition.[4]

Most philosophers who accept the distinction between sentences and propositions regard propositions and states of affairs as eternal entities. The truth-value of these eternal propositions never changes. If p is a proposition, then p has always existed and has always been either true or false. Like many philosophical doctrines, this view no doubt seems odd to anyone hearing it for the first time. It is a tribute to the philosophical art that so many apparently weird theories are not only accepted but become the objects of fierce devotion. To defend this theory of propositions is beyond the scope of this *introductory* discussion. So let me simply assume it is true and move on to notice, first, what appears to be a serious problem for the theory.

The claim that propositions (as distinct from sentences) are eternally true or false entities seems contradicted by propositions that contain a reference to time. Consider the sentence "Nash is now typing." At the moment, the statement is true. But it obviously ceases to be true the instant I lift my fingers from the keys and turn off the machine. Since the statement under consideration is sometimes true and usually false, how can one seriously maintain that propositions are eternally true? The answer lies in the fact that the example, "Nash is now typing," is too poorly framed to serve as the real proposition in question. The doctrine that propositions are eternally true requires any statement that is in effect "open" because of some reference to time or place to be "closed." This can be done by eliminating tensed verbs and making explicit any relevant information that may only have been implied in the original.

My original statement, "Nash is now typing," is what I have called an "open statement." It contains a temporal reference (the word *now*). In order to approximate the proposition we need, it is necessary to remove any reference to time in the verb and then close the statement by making explicit a reference to the precise time. And so we get something like: "Nash is (tenselessly) typing at 10:14 A.M. on April 12, 1981." This proposition corresponds to a particular state of affairs, namely, Nash's typing at 10:14 A.M. on April 12, 1981.

This state of affairs can be expressed in a wide variety of sentences just as our earlier state of affairs (John's being married to Mary) can be stated in different sentences. Some of these sentences can be correctly uttered by some people, but not by others. For example, I am the only

---

[4]For more on the relationship between propositions and states of affairs, see Alvin Plantinga, *God, Freedom and Evil* (New York: Harper and Row, 1974), pp. 34ff.

one who can refer to the state of affairs, Nash's typing, by writing, "I am typing at 10:14 A.M. on April 12, 1981." No one else, not even God, can correctly refer to this state of affairs by using the singular first-person pronoun. And, of course, the same state of affairs must be expressed in different sentences at different times. Someone who knows my plans for the day could say at 8 A.M. on April 12, "Nash will be typing at 10:14 today." Or at 10:14, he could see me working and truthfully say, "Nash is now typing." Or on April 13, he could say, "Nash was typing yesterday at 10:14 A.M." I see no problem in allowing that all these different utterances refer to the same piece of information, describe the same state of affairs. It is possible for two people to know the same piece of information even though they cannot express that knowledge with the same words. It is possible for the same person to know the same piece of information even though the inexorable march of time means that the tensed sentences used to express that information may change in truth-value.

The application of these points to my three sentences about the birth of Christ should now be obvious. All three sentences refer to the same state of affairs, Christ's being born. That some references to this state of affairs must use the present tense while others use the past or future tense must not mislead us into thinking that we are referring to different states of affairs. Once we recognize that the same piece of information can be expressed in different language, nothing in principle precludes the same person from knowing everything expressed in these different sentences at the same time.

To illustrate this, let us adopt the convention of allowing T_1, T_2, T_3, and so on to serve as variables for different times. Consider then each of the following lines:

God knows that at T_1, "Christ will be born" is true.
God knows that at T_1, "Christ is born" is false.
God knows that at T_1, "Christ was born" is false.

God knows that at T_2, "Christ is born" will be true.
God knows that at T_2, "Christ will be born" will be false.
God knows that at T_2, "Christ was born" will be false.

God knows that at T_3, "Christ was born" will be true.
God knows that at T_3, "Christ will be born" will be false.
God knows that at T_3, "Christ is born" will be false.

Undoubtedly, too much of this sort of thing can give philosophy a bad name. But in spite of its awkwardness, my analysis does show that the changing truth-value of the three statements about the birth of Christ does not entail that God's knowledge undergoes change. In chapter 8, "Immutability," I will discuss a possible sense in which a theist can speak of God's knowledge changing; it may even be that changes in God's conscious states are consistent with His immutabilit , in the most important senses of that ambiguous term. My point here is that nothing in the present discussion points to any unresolvable tension between omniscience and immutability. Nothing in principle precludes one person from knowing at one and the same time everything expressed by the three sentences. It is possible for God to know all of these points at the same time.

Suppose, to give one final example, that Mr. Jones knows that "today is Tuesday." Surely, someone else (Mr. Smith, for example) can know on a different day what Jones knew on Tuesday. On Wednesday, for example, Smith can say, "I know that yesterday, Jones knew it was Tuesday." A third person could report what Smith knew by saying, "On Wednesday, Smith knew that on the previous day, Jones knew it was then Tuesday." What all this shows is that even though Smith may have to use different language, he can know what Jones knew. Thus, the most the argument alleging an incompatibility between divine omniscience and immutability can show is that God may have to express His knowledge in language that differs from the language others might use. While this may be an interesting bit of information about God, it hardly qualifies as a reason to abandon belief in either God's omniscience or immutability.

OMNISCIENCE AND THE COHERENCE OF THEISM

In the article cited earlier in this chapter, Norman Kretzmann levelled still another argument against the coherence of theism. He argued that "the doctrine that God knows everything is incompatible . . . with theism, the doctrine of a personal God distinct from other persons."[5] Reflect a bit on the differences between the following statements:

(6) Nash knows that he is in Cherry Hall;
(7) Nash knows the statement "I am in Cherry Hall" is true;
(8) Mayhew knows that Nash is in Cherry Hall; and
(9) Mayhew knows the statement "Nash is in Cherry Hall" is true.

In all four cases, what is known is that Nash is in Cherry Hall. But because I am Nash and know that I am in Cherry Hall, the statements in quotes in (7) and (9) are logically independent. In principle, anyone might know what Mayhew is described as knowing in (8) and (9). But only Nash can know what (6) and (7) describe him as knowing. Every person knows propositions that are unknowable by any other person. Where "I" refers to the writer of this sentence, I am the only person

---

[5]Kretzmann, "Omniscience and Immutability," p. 420.

who, given the constancy of the referent of "I," knows that I am in Cherry Hall.

Kretzmann's application of this well-known fact to theology may surprise many readers. He assumes that if God is omniscient, God must know all these first-person indexical statements. But if God truly knows what Nash knows when Nash says "I am in Cherry Hall," it follows that God is identical with Nash; God is also identical with every other person who knows one of these first-person indexical statements. But if God is identical with all these other persons whose first-person accounts of knowledge He knows in the first-person, then the theistic concept of God as a Person distinct from created persons is false.

On the other hand, if we attempt to avoid this conclusion by saying that God cannot know what other persons know in their first-person indexical statements, it seems to follow that God is not omniscient. While God can have third-person knowledge about that of which Nash has first-person knowledge, God cannot know everything. God certainly cannot know what Nash knows when Nash knows he is in Cherry Hall. The only apparent way God could know what Nash is described as knowing in (6) and (7) is if God were identical with Nash. But identifying God with any of His creatures would deny a cardinal tenet of theism, namely, that God is a conscious person distinct from His creatures. So if theism is true, God cannot know what (6) and (7) describe Nash as knowing, a fact that allegedly compromises His omniscience. But if God does know (6) and (7) in the same way as Nash, then theism is false.

This argument turns out to be no better than the one studied in the first half of this chapter. While God's knowledge cannot always be expressed in the same sentences humans use, there is nothing to preclude His knowing the same pieces of information. The same state of affairs can be described in different words. The state of affairs or the information contained in "Nash knows that he is in Cherry Hall" can be contained in a third-person statement like (8) and (9). The subtle differences do not disqualify God or anybody else from knowing the same bit of information. God can know what we express in first-person statements even if it is impossible for Him or any other third person to express it in the same way. Kretzmann's line of argument, therefore, fails to demonstrate any logical incompatibility between the attributes of omniscience and immutability or between omniscience and the theist's belief in God as a personal being.[6]

---

[6]For Kretzmann's current position on the attributes of immutability and eternity, see Eleonore Stump and Norman Kretzmann, "Eternity," *Journal of Philosophy* 78 (1981): 429–58.

 Eternity

If the God of theism exists, He exists eternally. About this, there can be no disagreement. The major question that arises in connection with the eternity of God concerns how the attribute should be interpreted. According to most of the classical Christian theologians like Augustine, Anselm, and Aquinas, God's eternal existence is to be understood as *timelessness*. The doctrine of timelessness entails more than that God's existence is without beginning or end. It implies that God exists totally outside of time. God has neither temporal duration nor temporal location; God's existence does not occur during any period of time and He does not exist at any particular moment of time. God is "outside" of time. For a timeless God, all of time exists in one eternal present.

The timelessness doctrine originated in the philosophy of Plato, matured in the system of Neoplatonism, entered Christian thought through the Christian Platonism of Augustine, and held sway throughout the Middle Ages. It was challenged in the late Middle Ages by Duns Scotus and William of Occam but regained influence in both Roman Catholic and Protestant theology.

Other Christian thinkers subsequent to Duns Scotus and William of Occam have had second thoughts also about interpreting God's eternal existence as timelessness. In their view, it is preferable to say that God is *everlasting*. By this they mean that though God's existence has neither beginning nor end, it is a mistake to think of God as entirely divorced from the process of time.

The interpretation of God's eternal existence as everlastingness rather than timelessness can be found in Samuel Clarke's *A Demonstration of the Being and Attributes of God* (1705) and Jonathan Edwards's *Freedom of the Will* (1754). Contemporary proponents of this interpretation include Nelson Pike,[1] Nicholas Wolterstorff,[2] Richard Swinburne,[3] William Rowe,[4] and Anthony Kenny.[5] Theologians promoting the concept of everlastingness range from process theologians to neo-orthodox thinkers like Emil Brunner[6] to conservatives like J. Oliver Buswell, Jr.[7]

The debate as to which interpretation of God's eternity is best, is thought to hold significant implications for the doctrine of human free will and other aspects of Christian theology. It is often assumed, for example, that the timelessness doctrine makes it easier for the theist to reconcile divine foreknowledge and human freedom. Advocates of the timelessness doctrine have been put on the defensive in recent years as their position has come under attack from several directions. I will examine the five objections to timelessness that have been most prominent in the current debate. The first three are philosophical, while the last two are more closely related to biblical and theological issues.

THE PARADOXES OF TIMELESSNESS

One line of attack suggests that the notion of timelessness is incoherent because it gives rise to paradoxes. Anthony Kenny is one who has made this charge.

> Indeed, the whole concept of a timeless eternity, the whole of which is simultaneous with every part of time, seems to be radically incoherent. For simultaneity as ordinarily understood is a transitive relation. If A happens at the same time as B, and B happens at the same time as C, then A happens at the same time as C. If the BBC programme and the ITV programme both start when Big Ben strikes ten, then they both start at the same time. But, on St. Thomas' view, my typing of this paper is simultaneous with the whole of eternity. Again, on his view, the great fire of Rome is simultaneous with the whole of eternity. Therefore, while I type these very words, Nero fiddles heartlessly on.[8]

It would appear that any theory implying that yesterday is the same day

---

[1]Nelson Pike, *God and Timelessness* (New York: Schocken Books, 1970).

[2]Nicholas Wolterstorff, "God Everlasting," in *God and the Good*, ed. Clifton Orlebeke and Lewis Smedes (Grand Rapids: Eerdmans, 1975), pp. 181–203.

[3]Richard Swinburne, *The Coherence of Theism* (Oxford: Clarendon Press, 1977).

[4]William L. Rowe, *Philosophy of Religion* (Encino, Calif.: Dickenson Publishing Co., 1978).

[5]Anthony Kenny, *The God of the Philosophers* (Oxford: Clarendon Press, 1979).

[6]Emil Brunner, *The Christian Doctrine of God* (Philadelphia: Westminster, 1950), pp. 270–71.

[7]James Oliver Buswell, Jr., *A Systematic Theology of the Christian Religion*, 2 vols. (Grand Rapids: Zondervan, 1962), 1:43ff.

[8]Anthony Kenny, "Divine Foreknowledge and Human Freedom," in *Aquinas: A Collection of Critical Essays*, ed. A. Kenny (New York: Doubleday, 1969), p. 264.

as today and is also the same as tomorrow conflicts with the reality of temporal succession and is absurd.

A defender of timelessness might deal with this charge by replying that the critic of the doctrine fails to distinguish between viewing an event from the divine and the human perspectives. Defenders of the timelessness doctrine have resorted to several analogies in their effort to explain how two events might be related temporally in one sense and be simultaneous in another. While the points of a circle are related to each other in a particular order, all points maintain the same relation to the circle's center. The points of a circle can be interpreted as occupying the relationships of before, after, and simultaneous with. Even though point A might be prior to B and B subsequent to A, both points occupy the same relationship to the center of the circle. Using this analogy, the defender of timelessness might claim that though every temporal event has the same relationship to God's eternal present, God can still know that A comes before B and C comes after B. But obviously, no one living along the points of the circle, so to speak, could know what God knows from His position at the center of the circle. But this peculiar failing of finite humans hardly proves that this kind of knowledge is impossible. When Kenny argues that divine timelessness implies that two events hundreds of years apart are actually simultaneous, he commits a category mistake. His error is like that of a person who tries to argue that different points of a circle occur at the same point. This kind of mistake can only be made by someone who confuses the different relationships the points have to each other with the same relationship they have to the circle's center. Kenny's so-called paradox arises only because he mixes indiscriminately the human and divine perspectives.

A second analogy was utilized by both Augustine and Aquinas in their defense of the timelessness doctrine. They referred to the example of an observer on a high hill or tower who sees things going on far below him. Clearly, they thought, such an observer could be simultaneously aware of many different *spatial* relationships.[9] He could perceive that B is in front of A and that C is behind B. Even if the observer were separated from the spatial points, he could know the spatial relationships occupied by the things below him. Analogously, God can be outside of time and still know the temporal relationships between events; He knows that Nero's fiddling takes place after Paul's conversion. While God will not know anything as future for Himself, He will still be able to know that something is future for Paul or Nero or someone else. Teske's summary of this analogy is helpful.

---

[9]Some critics of the analogy overlook the fact that what is being compared is the observer's ability to behold several *spatial* relationships in one glance with God's knowledge of many *temporal* relationships.

Aquinas says that God is outside the order of time and this can be illustrated by someone outside of an order of places. For example, a road is an ordered set of places. Hence, someone on the road is in the ordered set of places. Others on the road are either ahead of him, alongside him, or behind him. However, for someone outside of the particular ordered set of places, e.g., for someone on a mountain top that overlooks the stretch of road, the travelers on the road are seen in one glance as before or alongside or after one another, but not as before or alongside or after the viewer from the mountain. Yet the viewer on the mountain is, nonetheless, spatially related to the travelers on the road, even though, because he is not on the road, i.e, because he is outside of that particular order of places, he is not before or alongside or after any of the travelers on the road. Now God, according to Aquinas, is not merely outside of a particular order of time, but outside of time. Hence, as outside of time, God's vision can take in the whole temporal order of events; his vision sees the whole order of events occurring successively in the temporal order. However, his knowledge is not before or simultaneous with or after any event in the order of temporal succession, though each successive event in the order of time is present to his eternal vision.[10]

A third analogy that is helpful in conceptualizing some of the differences between timeless and temporal relationships is a work of fiction, say, a novel. Once the novel is completed, the author has a different relationship to the sequence of events in the novel than someone reading it for the first time. The reader encounters a series of events in chronological order. But there is a sense in which the author of the novel has a simultaneous overview of all the events. To the author, the entire book is in his present, in a manner of speaking. He could have written the end before the beginning. But in order to follow the story, the reader must read the book sequentially and thus perceive how what is future for the characters in chapter four becomes a part of their past in chapter six. Because two perspectives (that of the author and the reader) can be distinguished, two kinds of experience of temporal sequence exist. Something similar may exist in the relationship that movie directors have to their completed motion picture. The person viewing the film for the first time must experience the recorded events in a certain chronological sequence. But there is an obvious sense in which a director, who is in total control of his film from the beginning, knows every scene in his present.

All of the analogies I have noted run into difficulty if pushed too far. But they all have one merit, namely, showing that some sense can be made of the claim that the same events can be viewed from such

[10]Roland H. Teske, S.J., "Omniscience, Omnipotence and Divine Transcendence," *The New Scholasticism* 53 (1979): 293. See Aquinas, *Summa Theologica* I, 14, 13 *ad* 3.

radically different perspectives that they must be described with different temporal predicates. It is not at all clear that the doctrine of timelessness suffers from the kind of incoherence suggested by the so-called paradoxes of timelessness.

TIMELESSNESS AND THE NOTION OF PROPHECY

Anthony Kenny is also the source for our next objection against timelessness. He writes:

> An argument *ad hominem* against St. Thomas' position may be drawn from the notion of prophecy. St. Thomas believed that God could foretell, and had foretold, future contingent events. He believed, for example, that God, as the principal author of the Epistle to the Romans, had foretold the conversion of the Jewish people to Christianity. On the view that God's knowledge is timeless, such prediction becomes inexplicable. For, if God's knowledge is timeless, then we cannot attach to statements about God's knowledge such adverbial clauses as "at the time when the Epistle to the Romans was written." We cannot, for example, say "At the time when the Epistle to the Romans was written God already knew that the Jews would finally be converted." But if God did not then know it, how could He then foretell it? To put it bluntly; if God did not then *know* that the Jews would be converted, He had no right then to *say* that they would.[11]

Paul Helm finds Kenny's admittedly *ad hominem* argument unconvincing. He believes it can be countered by the simple claim that biblical prophecy expresses "what a temporal agent may, at a particular time, truly say that God timelessly knows."[12] Certainly it is true that at the time the Epistle to the Romans was being written, God already knew that the Jews would be saved. But, Helm insists, this means simply that the statement "God timelessly knows when the Jew will be converted" was true at a time prior to the writing of the epistle. No inconsistency exists. Statements about prophecy and what a timeless being "foreknows" can be viewed as reports of what a temporal agent recognizes about a timeless being's knowledge. In other words, words like *prophesy* or verbs in the future tense may be applied to the way in which temporal agents know something but would be misleading if used to describe the way in which God knows something.

TIMELESSNESS AND KNOWLEDGE OF
TIMELESS TRUTHS

The late British philosopher, Arthur Prior, has contended that the timelessness doctrine would restrict God's knowledge to timeless truths.

---

[11]Kenny, "Divine Foreknowledge and Human Freedom," p. 263.
[12]Paul Helm, "Timelessness and Foreknowledge," *Mind* 84 (1975): 524.

> God could not, on the view I am considering, know that the 1960 final examinations at Manchester are now over; for this isn't something that He or anyone could know timelessly, because it just isn't true timelessly. . . . So far as I can see all that can be said on this subject timelessly is that the finishing-date of the 1960 final examinations is an earlier one than 29th August, and this is *not* the thing we know when we know that those examinations are over.[13]

In other words, Prior believed the timelessness doctrine severely restricts the knowledge of God to such a degree that God could know only timeless truths like "three plus five equals eight." A timeless God could not know any of the myriad of temporal truths that any temporal being can know. Few have been persuaded by Prior's argument. Anthony Kenny, himself a critic of the timelessness theory, has observed that Prior has "not in fact identified a range of facts that a timeless being could not know, but only certain forms of words that a timeless individual could not use when formulating or reporting his knowledge."[14] Kenny suggests that a timeless being could report information about temporal facts in statements that did not include temporal indexical expressions.

Paul Helm makes much the same point. He offers an illustration of how a timeless being might describe Prior's claim about the 1960 final exams at Manchester being now over.

> Another thing that could be known timelessly is that the 1960 final examinations at Manchester are over for Prior in 1961, but not over for Prior in 1960. A timeless being could even know (at some cost to ordinary language, but quite perspicuously) that (say) the 15th June examination is *now* for Prior on the 15th June, and was then (past) for Prior on the 16th June.[15]

Helm faults Prior for not distinguishing more carefully between sentences and propositions.

> The proposition that is expressed by Prior by "The examination is now over" when uttered on a particular occasion can be expressed in various other ways. . . . But if the expressing of the same proposition by various sentences is allowed, then there seems to be no reason why indexicals should not be replaced by dates and places.[16]

Helm's point is that though a timeless being may be precluded from expressing what he knows in sentences identical to those a temporal

---

[13]Arthur Prior, "The Formalities of Omniscience," in Prior's *Papers on Time and Tense* (London: Oxford University Press, 1968), p. 29. Prior's paper appeared originally in the April 1962 issue of *Philosophy*.

[14]Kenny, *God of the Philosophers*, pp. 39–40.

[15]Helm, "Timelessness and Foreknowledge," p. 517.

[16]Ibid., p. 518.

being would use, still the timeless being can affirm the same proposition or meaning in different language.

A similar response is given by Nelson Pike. Pike acknowledges that a timeless being "could not have an item of knowledge that *he* could formulate or report in a statement such as . . 'Today is the twelfth of May.' This is because statements of this sort serve (in part) to identify the temporal position of the speaker relative to some event or circumstance."[17] But Pike "cannot see, however, that this observation gives warrant for the claim that there is something that a timeless individual could not know."[18] The most that Prior has established, Pike believes, "is that there are certain *forms of words* that a timeless individual could not use when formulating or reporting his knowledge."[19] This third philosophical objection to timelessness, thus, seems to fare no better than the first two. Two theological objections to the doctrine, however, may raise more serious problems.

TIMELESSNESS AND DIVINE ACTS IN TIME

Nelson Pike maintains that the doctrine of timelessness is incompatible with such pivotal Christian doctrines as God's creation and preservation of the world. Every verb that might be used to refer to God's creating and sustaining activities ("God makes," "God brings into existence," "God preserves," etc.) contains an unavoidable temporal reference. References to creation necessarily refer to something that happened in the past; accounts of God's sustaining activity refer to something continuing over a period of time. According to Pike, if the verbs used to describe God's creative and sustaining activity have a temporal dimension, then God's activity must be in time. And if God's activity is in time, then God must be in time since God cannot be separated from His acts.[20]

Pike also argues that the notion of timelessness is incompatible with a belief in God as a person. The most important acts which we normally expect a person to be able to perform (remembering, anticipating, reflecting, deliberating, intending, etc.) are acts that a timeless God could not perform, according to Pike. Remembering is an activity that necessarily involves a relationship to the past; intending is apparently an impossible act for a being for whom there is no future. If God is capable of forgiving, His forgiveness must apply to human actions that have already occurred, that belong to the past. If God promises anything, His activity must have the future in view. Divorce God from

[17]Pike, *God and Timelessness*, pp. 94–95.
[18]Ibid., p. 95.
[19]Ibid.
[20]Ibid., chap. 6.

time, then, and He becomes a being incapable of performing most of the acts essential to personhood.[21] The view that God is not a person is clearly inconsistent with Christian theism.

E. L. Mascall addressed the issues raised by this set of objections in his book, *The Openness of Being*.[22] He agreed that many biblical statements describe actions of God within time. God's delivering Israel from Egypt and raising Jesus from the dead were certainly temporal events. Nevertheless, Mascall insisted that the defender of timelessness can avoid Pike's problems by noting that the acts of God have two poles, a subjective pole that is timeless and an objective pole that is temporal. As Mascall put it, the act of God is,

> at its subjective pole (at God's end, if we may use the phrase), timeless, even though at its objective pole (at the creature's end) it is temporal. God timelessly exerts a creative activity towards and upon the whole spatio-temporal fabric of the created universe. This will be experienced as temporal by each creature who observes it and describes it from his own spatio-temporal standpoint; but it no more implies that God is in time . . . than the fact that I describe God in English means that God is English.[23]

Then Mascall switches from defense to offense.

> The act in which God both preserves and knows the finite universe must necessarily be timeless and spaceless, since its object is the totality of spatio-temporal existence. If it is asserted that, in spite of this, there must be in God's own mode of existence something analogous to time, we can only reply that this must in fact be God's eternity and that what differentiates it from time is the absence of change and succession.[24]

He then continues:

> Just because time and change are genuinely inherent in the finite world and are not just an ocean in which it floats or a backcloth against which it casts its shadows, its transcendent Creator must transcend its temporality as he transcends all its other limitations. A god to whom, in his timelessness, the whole spatio-temporal fabric of the world is eternally present is not less but more concerned with the world and its affairs than would be a God who was entangled in it. For the latter kind of deity would be limited in his experience at each moment to the particular stage in its development that the world had reached at that moment, while the former, in his extra-temporal and extra-spatial vision and activity, embraces in one timeless act every one of his creatures whatever its time and place may be. Difficult, and indeed impossible, as it is for us to imagine and feel what timeless existence is like, we can, I think, understand that a God to whom

---

[21]Ibid., chap. 7. A similar argument is found in Swinburne's *The Coherence of Theism*, p. 221.

[22]E. L. Mascall, *The Openness of Being* (Philadelphia: Westminster, 1971).

[23]Ibid., p. 166.

[24]Ibid., p. 168.

every instant is present at once has a vastly greater scope for his compassion and his power than one would have who could attend to only one moment at a time. Thus, in emphasising the timelessness of God, we are not conceiving him as remote but quite the opposite. [25]

Unfortunately, Mascall's attempt to strengthen the timelessness doctrine includes some distortion of the view he opposes. True, if an everlasting God were forced to attend to but one moment at a time, problems might arise about His omniscience. And if an everlasting God were "entangled" with the temporal world, serious questions might be raised about His omnipotence. But a defender of the view of God as everlasting may insist, quite consistently, that God is still Lord over time and can still behold all time simultaneously. [26]

TIMELESSNESS AND THE DIVINE TIME-STRAND

Nicholas Wolterstorff rejects the timelessness doctrine because it comes into unavoidable conflict, he thinks, with the clear teaching of Scripture. According to Wolterstorff, the Redeemer-God of the Scriptures cannot be a timeless God because a redeeming God is one who changes. Wolterstorff claims that the key element of any temporal process is an ordering relation in which there is a before, a present, and an after. In order for something to be timeless, none of these ordering relationships can be applicable to that being. If a being is truly timeless, it should be impossible for it to exist simultaneously with anything else, or before anything else, or after anything else. Once it is established that a being does occupy one of these ordering relations, then that being is clearly temporal.

Wolterstorff thinks it evident that

the biblical writers regard God as having a time-strand of his own on which actions on his part are to be found, and that some at least of these actions vary in such a way that there are changes along the strand. It seems evident that they do not regard changes on time-strands as confined to entities in God's creation. The God who acts, in the way in which the biblical writers speak of God as acting, seems clearly to change. [27]

If one's view of God is derived from Scripture, Wolterstorff insists, "Temporality embraces us along with God."[28] But this fact does not compromise God's Lordship.

Though God is within time, yet he is Lord of time. The whole array of contingent temporal events is within his power. He is Lord of what occurs.

---

[25]Ibid., pp. 171–72.
[26]See Wolterstorff, "God Everlasting."
[27]Ibid., p. 193.
[28]Ibid., p. 202.

And that, along with the specific pattern of what he does, grounds all authentically biblical worship of, and obedience to, God. It is not because he is outside of time—eternal, immutable, impassive—that we are to worship and obey God. It is because of what he can and does bring about within time that we mortals are to render him praise and obedience.[29]

Even if a theist wishes to maintain that God's "time" is not our time, it is still true that God has His own time-strand along which events occupy temporal relationships. The Exodus came before the Crucifixion and the Ascension came after the Resurrection. Wolterstorff seems to think that the whole timelessness doctrine is misguided because it places its emphasis at the wrong point. It confuses the fact of God's being Lord over what happens within time with God's being outside of time. It assumes that if God is in time, He cannot be Lord of what occurs in time. The timelessness of God and the sovereignty of God are clearly independent notions. The gods of Plato and Aristotle were timeless but they were not the Lord of creation. Wolterstorff's essay is a plea to advocates of classical theism to place their emphasis where it belongs, on the sovereignty of God. God's sovereignty is not compromised in any way by the Scriptures' assertion that God acts in time and is thus an everlasting being.

CONCLUSION

Many thinkers have changed their minds about the two interpretations of God's eternal existence. Richard Swinburne, for example, wrote two articles in 1965 for the *Christian Quarterly Review* defending the timelessness doctrine.[30] By 1973, Swinburne was expressing serious doubts about the intelligibility and coherence of the theory.[31] And when he finally published *The Coherence of Theism* in 1977, he repudiated his 1965 articles and rejected divine timelessness.[32]

A philosopher who has changed his thinking in the other direction is Paul Helm. Several years ago he seemed very skeptical about the timelessness theory.[33] But in his most recent article on the subject,

---

[29]Ibid., p. 203.

[30]Richard Swinburne, "The Timelessness of God, I," *Christian Quarterly Review*, 1965, pp. 323–37 and part II, also in the 1965 volume, 472–87.

[31]See Richard Swinburne, "Omnipotence," *American Philosophical Quarterly* 10 (1973): 236.

[32]*The Coherence of Theism*, p. 218.

[33]Paul Helm, "Timelessness and Foreknowledge," *Mind* 84 (1975): 516–27. See also Helm's "God and Whatever Comes to Pass," *Religious Studies* 14 (1978): 315–23.

Helm argues that divine timelessness may be as important to theism as divine spacelessness.[34]

Many readers will expect this chapter to reach a definite conclusion on the subject of God's relation to time. Is God a timeless or an everlasting being? At this time, I don't know. Like many theists, there was a time when I simply took the timelessness doctrine for granted. After all, it had a long and honored history and did offer a solution to problems like the apparent conflict between divine foreknowledge and human freedom. I then passed through a stage where my confidence in the theory wavered. Some pretty impressive arguments, I thought, had been raised against it. But I no longer find many of those arguments so overpowering. Helm's claim that the doctrines of spacelessness and timelessness logically hang together may constitute the strongest argument for timelessness yet offered. But the jury is still out and presently I see no reason why theism cannot accommodate itself to either interpretation.[35]

---

[34]Paul Helm, "God and Spacelessness," *Philosophy* 55 (1980): 221. Helm's latest point is worth noticing: "In saying that we ought to conclude that if God exists he is outside space and time I am by no means claiming that I fully understand what these propositions amount to. Perhaps the best way to grasp what they mean, or to try to grasp what they mean, is to use models or analogies. And then again, perhaps not. All that I am claiming is that the spacelessness of God seems to be a requirement of traditional theism and hence that the timelessness of God does."

[35]As we know, misery loves company. For examples of the indecisiveness of other writers on this subject, see Pike's *God and Timelessness*, p. 190; and Stewart R. Sutherland, "God, Time and Eternity," *Proceedings of the Aristotelian Society* 79 (1978–1979): 103–21.

Chapter 7

Simplicity

The doctrine of divine simplicity has a public relations problem. Few people have even heard that God supposedly has the property of simplicity. Fewer still have any idea what the doctrine entails or why theologians have thought it necessary to ascribe the property to God. The doctrine of simplicity is the belief that God is identical with His nature or His properties. Another aspect of the theory teaches that God's essence is indivisible in the sense that God's properties are not *parts* of God's nature. Simplicity is therefore said to be unique to God; it marks off one of the fundamental differences between God's nature and human nature.

Once we state that God's essence has no parts, however, a problem arises. Human beings could never have knowledge of an absolutely simple essence. To avoid skepticism that would result, many advocates of divine simplicity believe, with Lutheran theologian Francis Pieper, that "since finite human reason cannot comprehend the infinite and absolute simplex, God condescends to our weakness and in His Word divides Himself, as it were into a number of attributes which our faith can grasp and to which it can cling."[1] In other words, because human beings are incapable of comprehending God's nature because of its absolute simplicity, God makes a concession to human fallibility and, in His revelation, "divides" his simple being into "parts" (the various attributes) in order to enable us to comprehend Him.

The interpretation of simplicity given by thinkers like Pieper implies that the properties theologians usually identify as divine attributes are not *objective*, that is, do not exist as real distinctions within the being of God. The attributes are *subjective* in the sense that they exist as features of the way in which human beings conceive the indivisible

---

[1]Francis Pieper, *Christian Dogmatics*, 4 vols. (St. Louis: Concordia, 1951), 1:428.

essence of God. Many theologians insist, however, that the different properties by which human beings apprehend the nature of God have some objective basis in the divine nature.

The most influential statement of the doctrine of simplicy is found in the writings of Thomas Aquinas.[2] Frederick Copleston provides a helpful summary:

> The attributes of God are not really distinct from one another, since God is simple: they are identical with the divine essence. The divine intelligence is not really distinct from the divine essence, nor is the divine will. . . If we could comprehend the divine essence as it is in itself and if we could give it its proper name, we should use one alone. We cannot, however, comprehend the divine essence, and we know it only by means of diverse concepts: we have, therefore to employ diverse words to express the divine essence, though we know at the same time that the actual reality corresponding to all those names is one simple reality.[3]

But this theory too raises a serious question. If human beings necessarily conceive God differently than He really is, is their conception of God not therefore false? Copleston's answer is no,

> for we know that God is actually a simple Being, but we conceive in a composite manner the object which we know to be non-composite. This means that our intelligences are finite and discursive and that they cannot apprehend God save by means of His different reflections in creatures. Our knowledge of God is thus inadequate and imperfect, but it is not false. *There is indeed a certain foundation in God for our composite and distinct concepts*, this foundation, however, not being any real distinction in God between the divine attributes but simply His infinite perfection which precisely because of its infinite richness, cannot be apprehended by the human mind in one concept.[4]

But perhaps I have not yet made the issues raised by the doctrine of simplicity sufficiently clear. An understanding of the medieval background may provide a helpful starting point for eliminating some of the confusions we have encountered.

THE MEDIEVAL DEBATE OVER SIMPLICITY

Several features of the doctrine of simplicity resulted from attempts to avoid two extreme movements that were considered threats to Christian theology during the Middle Ages: extreme realism (or hyperreal-

---

[2]See *Summa Theologica*, part I, question 3.
[3]Frederick Copleston, *History of Philosophy*, 8 vols. (Westminster, Maryland: Newman, 1962), 2:360–61.
[4]Ibid., p. 361.

ism) and nominalism.[5] These labels identify differing interpretations adopted by medieval philosphers with regard to the so-called problem of universals which had resulted from reflection on entities Plato had called forms or ideas. Plato had taught that for every class concept (universal) there exists something (some particular) that corresponds to that concept. Consider, for example, any sentence of the form S is P (where S is any subject and P is any property) and substitute for P any one of a countless number of predicates like red, true, tall, square, and so on. Because such predicates can be applied to a large number of particular things, they came to be known as universal terms. The predicate *red* is a universal inasmuch as the word can denote innumerable particular instances of the color.* Several basic questions were asked about such universals: do they exist only in the mind or can they exist apart from the mind? Are they corporeal or incorporeal?

Philosophers who held that universals, like properties, really do exist apart from the particular things that exemplify them came to be known as realists. Thinkers who disagreed came to be called nominalists because, for the most part, they suggested that universals were nothing more than words (Latin: *nomina*). For any bona fide nominalist, properties (even the properties of God) do not exist. Only particular things exist.

A small group of realists insisted on taking the Platonic belief in the existence of properties, relations, and numbers to an extreme position that created serious problems for Christian theology. Carried away in their enthusiasm for universals, these extreme realists (or hyper-realists) minimized the importance of particulars to the extent that they seemed to deny the differences between particular things. The universal became everything, while individual particulars faded into ontological oblivion. One hyper-realist, William of Champeaux, reportedly went so far as to deny the doctrine of the Trinity. According to medieval discussions of his position, William so exaggerated the unity of the Godhead that he appeared to deny the distinctions between the divine persons.

The threat that extreme realism posed to the Christian doctrine of God resulted from its tendency to take properties like wisdom and goodness and hypostatize them into existing entities. With respect to the properties of God, the problem was obvious. If the properties or attributes of God are hypostatized existents, then God is a composite

---

[5]Because the same movements challenged Judaism and Islam, the doctrine of simplicity also is prominent in the writings of Jewish and Islamic thinkers during the Middle Ages.

*More specifically, examples of universals include properties (like redness) and relations (like similarity and betweenness). But also of concern are the existence of entities like numbers and propositions.

being. In other words, the extreme realists took properties such as being wise, being powerful, and being good and turned them into substances like wisdom, power, and goodness. This effectively made God's nature a construct of more basic building blocks, namely, the hypostatized attributes.

It is easy to see the threat medieval theists saw in this theory. Each of the theological utterances about simplicity can be seen as a conscious effort to avoid the absurdities of a hyper-realistic position:

> We must thus not conceive of the attributes as if they would make a composite of the simple being of God.[6]

> We must not represent God as a composite being, composed of different elements.[7]

> By this we mean that there is no composition of any kind in the Divine Being.[8]

Viewed against the background of the perceived threat from extreme realism, some features of the doctrine of simplicity begin to make sense.[9] Theological claims that God is not composed of parts are attempts to avoid the absurd or heretical implications of a hyper-realist interpretation of the divine attributes.

While extreme realism menaced Christianity by making God's being into a composite, nominalism, the second threat to the medieval doctrine of God, went to the opposite extreme and denied any differences among the divine attributes. The nominalist argument took the following form:

1. Universals do not exist.
2. Therefore, properties (a species of universals) do not exist.
3. Therefore, God does not have any properties; God has no nature.
4. Therefore, words that apparently refer to divine attributes cannot possibly denote distinguishable properties within the divine essence. There are no properties of God to which they can refer.*

---

[6]Hendrikus Berkhof, *Christian Faith*, trans. Sierd Woudstra (Grand Rapids: Eerdmans, 1979), p. 116.

[7]Charles Hodge, *Systematic Theology*, 3 vols. (Grand Rapids: Eerdmans, 1965), 1:369.

[8]Herman Bavinck, *The Doctrine of God* (Grand Rapids: Baker, 1977), p. 168.

[9]Consider Bavinck's claim: "By means of this doctrine of God's simplicity Christian theology was kept from falling into the error of regarding God's attributes as separate from and more or less independent of his essence." Ibid., p. 121.

*This step had the advantage of eliminating in one fell swoop all of the problems raised by the extreme realists. It is no longer possible to think of God as composed of parts (viz., the attributes) since the "parts" do not exist.

5. Since words referring to divine attributes all have the same referent (nothing), all of God's attribute-words mean the same thing.
6. Thus, absolutely no differences exist between the various attributes of God.
7. Thus, God's omniscience is identical with His omnipotence, which is identical with His goodness, and so on.

For nominalism, which denied the existence of properties, the only things that exist are particular things. Universals are simply words to which no actually existing thing corresponds. Since properties do not exist, it follows that God cannot have properties; therefore, God has no nature. Given a nominalistic analysis of the alleged properties of God, "wisdom," "truth," and "power" are just words. Since there is no *real* distinction between the referents of these terms, the difference between them is basically a verbal difference; nothing in reality is denoted by such words. According to Berkhof, nominalists like William of Occam regarded the divine attributes as nothing more than *nomina* ("words") "referring to the various works of God, grounded not in God's objective reality . . . but only in the subjective human conception."[10] Bavinck adds:

> According to the Nominalists, especially according to Occam, the attributes differed only "in subjective reason, having a connotation with respect to diverse effects"; i.e., with a view to the relation which they severally assume to the works of God. The concept of any one attribute was held to be included in that of any other attribute. "The one is involved in the other." Hence, according to this reasoning when we ascribe goodness to God, we thereby ascribe to him justice, power, etc.[11]

Some nominalist conclusions sound suspiciously similar to the views of Francis Pieper. Many Lutheran theologians like Pieper deny any real distinction between the attributes. Since the influence of Occam's nominalism on the thought of Martin Luther is well known, it is easy to interpret the reappearance of some of these ideas as evidence of a continuing nominalist influence on Lutheran theology.

This nominalist influence may also explain the presence of a subjectivistic interpretation of the divine attributes in such Lutheran thinkers as Friedrich Schleiermacher and Paul Tillich. According to Schleiermacher, the divine attributes are nothing but effects that God has within human beings. God's holiness, for example, is nothing more than our feeling of guilt. According to Paul Tillich, omnipotence is a feeling of finitude that we all have in the presence of nonbeing. Immu-

---

[10]Berkhof, *Christian Faith*, p. 116.
[11]Bavinck, *Doctrine of God*, p. 128.

tability is the feeling of finitude we have in the presence of a deity whom we trust. More conservative Lutherans like Pieper would undoubtedly object to the extreme subjectivizing of Schleiermacher and Tillich. But Schleiermacher and Tillich could reply that they simply took the nominalist thesis to its inevitable conclusion. Unless there is some objective ground for a distinction between the divine attributes, what is to keep theologians from the position represented by Schleiermacher and Tillich? An objectivistic alternative to nominalism would insist that there is something within the divine essence which provides a ground for attributing the various properties to God. Something objective about God's being makes it proper to speak of Him as immutable or omnipotent.

The following quotations express the theological concern to avoid the errors of the nominalist position:

> We must not confound the attributes, making them all mean the same thing, which is equivalent to denying them altogether.[12]

> To say, as the schoolmen, and so many even of Protestant theologians, ancient and modern, were accustomed to say, that the divine attributes differ only in name, or in our conceptions, or in their effects, is to destroy all true knowledge of God.[13]

> If in God eternity is identical with knowledge, knowledge with power, power with ubiquity, and ubiquity with holiness, we are using words without meaning when we attribute any perfection to God. We must, therefore, either give up the attempt to determine the divine attributes from our speculative idea of an infinite essence, or renounce all knowledge of God, and all faith in the revelation of Himself, which He has made in the constitution of our nature, in the external world, and in his Word. Knowledge is no more identical with power in God than it is in us.[14]

The different attributes, on this view, must be distinguished in some objective way and not just within the human subject. Divine wisdom is not the same as divine power. It is also important that the attributes be viewed as having some basis in the divine nature.

To summarize the medieval debate, many of the odd-seeming statements in formulations of the doctrine of simplicity can be explained as attempts by representatives of the three major forms of theism (Christianity, Judaism, and Islam) to steer a middle course between two extreme medieval positions that were viewed as theologically dangerous:

---

[12]Hodge, *Systematic Theology*, p. 369.
[13]Ibid., p. 371.
[14]Ibid., p. 372.

extreme realism and nominalism.[15] Medieval advocates of simplicity believed that responsible thinking about God should avoid two errors: either thinking of God as a being composed of parts, or obliterating the distinctions between the divine attributes. With respect to the essence of God, theologians should neither divide the substance (the error of extreme realism) nor confuse the attributes (the mistake of the nominalists). We must neither divide God's essence into different parts (the hypostatized attributes), nor confuse the attributes so as to imply that there are no differences between them.

A CONTEMPORARY ANALYSIS OF SIMPLICITY

In a recent book, Alvin Plantinga has shown that the doctrine of simplicity appears to be required for a reason other than merely to rebut the extreme realism of the Middle Ages.[16] Plantinga asks us to suppose that God has a certain property like goodness. It is then the case either that the property of goodness "depends upon" God or it does not. Let us consider the first of these alternatives—that divine properties like goodness depend in some sense upon God. What might this mean? On any normal analysis, it would mean that God's existence preceded the existence of goodness; that God created goodness. But surely this cannot be. For if God's existence antedated that of goodness (or any other divine property), there would then have been a time when God was not good. And if this were so, it would mean that goodness is not an essential property of God. But God has always been good. (One of the things that is meant when we say something is an attribute of God is that God possesses that property essentially. And as the discussion in chapter 1 made clear, if something is an essential property of God, it is impossible for God to exist without that property.) Therefore, the theist must apparently reject the view that God's properties depend on Him, since it is incompatible with the belief that God's attributes are *essential* properties.

To repeat, either God's properties have always existed or God created them. But if God created His properties, there was a time when He did not possess those properties. And if this were so, then properties like goodness, justice, and wisdom could not be essential properties of God.

But if, on the other hand, God has always been good, then there seems to be a sense in which God depends on His properties; His existence seems conditioned or limited in some sense by His properties.

---

[15]However, as I have also pointed out, some contemporary formulations of the doctrine evidence an inordinate amount of nominalist influence.

[16]Alvin Plantinga, *Does God Have a Nature?* (Milwaukee: Marquette University Press, 1980).

God could not be good unless goodness existed. That God has essentially a property like goodness is something that is beyond His control. Moreover, the belief that God has a nature (properties) seems to limit God in other ways. Each of God's essential properties has characteristics that are beyond God's control. However goodness is defined, it will have specific characteristics that distinguish it. But the fact that goodness has these characteristics is not within God's control. Nothing God can do can make goodness be other than it is.

What Plantinga's argument makes clear is that the divine attributes themselves raise problems for theism, quite apart from any commitment to extreme realism. The apparently innocent beliefs that properties exist and that God has a nature (that is, that God possesses certain properties essentially) seem logically incompatible with the belief that God is sovereign (that is, that everything is under His control). As we have seen, if God has even one property, that property must have some kind of existence independent of God. Even the character of that property is independent of God. And, finally, there *is* a sense in which God's very existence depends upon His properties. Both the existence and the character of God's essential properties are, as Plantinga puts it, "necessary conditions of God's being the way *he* is."[17] Thus, the apparently innocent suggestion that God has a nature appears to conflict with a belief in the sovereignty of God. God's sovereignty seems limited by the fact that He has a nature.

The problems continue. If God is essentially good, then it is impossible for God not to be good. It is impossible for God to decide to be evil, even for a short while. Being nongood simply is not within God's power. God is good and He is stuck with that.

These observations appear to pose the Christian theist with a dilemma: either surrender the sovereignty of God (the belief that everything depends upon God) or reject the claim that God has a nature. If God is sovereign, then, it would appear He can have no essential properties. But if God has a nature (that is, if He has at least one essential property), then He cannot be sovereign.

Three ways of escape from this dilemma have been tried. According to the first, found in the philosophy of Descartes, God does have properties but He possesses none of them essentially. That is, God might have lacked any property He possesses, or He might have possessed some complementary property. Plantinga explains:

> On Descartes' view, then, God has no nature—not, indeed, because there are no properties to have, but because none of his properties is *essential* to him. There is no property he could not have lacked; if every

---

[17]Ibid., p. 7.

proposition is within his control, then every proposition predicating a property of him is within his control.[18]

Plantinga finds Descartes's total capitulation to the thesis of divine sovereignty "wildly counterintuitive."[19] It means that God

> could have brought it about . . . that he was powerless, without knowledge, and wicked. Indeed he could have brought it about that he was powerless, without knowledge, and wicked, but at the same time omnipotent, omniscient and morally perfect. . . . He could have brought it about that he does not exist while serenely continuing as a necessary being.[20]

Descartes's strange view would imply that both theism and atheism could be true at the same time. Descartes's claim that God does not have a nature stumbles over the simple fact that God does have at least one essential property, namely, the property of not knowing that He does not exist. And since God has at least this one essential property, He has a nature. But, Plantinga adds, God obviously has many more essential properties. Descartes's attempt to escape the dilemma fails.

Another attempt to evade the dilemma (either God is not sovereign or God does not have a nature) is offered by the contemporary nominalist. As we have seen, nominalists deny the existence of properties and other abstract entities. The nominalist simply accepts one horn of the dilemma: God cannot have a nature for the simple reason that there are no properties. "The nominalist doesn't hold that God is not omniscient; indeed he is, but there's no such thing as the property of omniscience. The truth that God is omniscient doesn't imply that there is some property—omniscience, for example—that God has."[21] Plantinga concludes that nominalism does not help at all for the basic reason that abstract entities like propositions and properties *do* exist. Even the nominalist believes there are truths or falsehoods.

> Even if there are no such things as the properties of being red and being colored, it is still true and necessarily true that whatever is red is colored; that truth is not within God's control. Perhaps there's no such thing as the color red; it still won't be up to God whether it's possible that there be red things. . . . Perhaps there's no such thing as the abstract object *All men are mortal*, or any other proposition. It remains necessarily true that if all men are mortal, then it's false that some men are not mortal; and this truth is not within God's control. Even if there is no such thing as the property *omniscience*, it remains true that God is omniscient, so that the truth *God is omniscient* isn't within his control. . . . If there are any necessary truths

---

[18]Ibid., p. 126.
[19]Ibid., p. 127.
[20]Ibid.
[21]Ibid., p. 63.

and if they are pretty much the ones we think they are, then there will be about as many truths outside God's control on the nominalist view as on the realist view.[22]

In other words, insofar as it is an attempt to preserve God's sovereign control over all things, nominalism is irrelevant. No matter how the theistic nominalist slices it, a great many things remain outside of God's control.

The doctrine of divine simplicity as formulated by Aquinas is the third way of escape from this dilemma. Aquinas sought to preserve both beliefs—that God has a nature and that God is sovereign. To this end he argued that God is identical with His nature. In God, essence and attribute are identical. On this view, it is misleading to suggest that God's properties are something that He has or possesses. God does not *have* the properties of goodness, wisdom, and justice. God *is* goodness, wisdom, and justice. Plantinga thinks Aquinas's theory raises some awkward problems for the Christian theist. Aquinas's position appears incompatible with at least two fundamental concerns of Christianity.

First, equating God with each of His properties entails that each of God's properties is identical with His other properties. If A is identical with B and if B is identical with C, then A is identical with C. Clearly, then, if God is identical with His property of knowledge and also identical with His property of perfect goodness, it then follows that the property of knowledge is identical with the property of perfect goodness. If each of God's properties is identical with all of God's other properties, the obvious conclusion to be drawn is that God has only one property. But this is mystifying, to say the least. While obviously there are many things about God that human beings may be incapable of comprehending, one of the things we do seem to know very clearly is that power and love and knowledge and mercy are not identical properties.

Second, Plantinga argues that Aquinas's doctrine of simplicity conflicts with the Christian belief that God is a person.

> If God is identical with each of his properties, then, since each of his properties is a property, he is a property—a self-exemplifying property. Accordingly God has just one property: himself. This view is subject to a difficulty both obvious and overwhelming. No property could have created the world; no property could be omniscient, or, indeed, know anything at all. If God is a property, then he isn't a person but a mere abstract object; he has no knowledge, awareness, power, love or life. So taken, the simplicity doctrine seems an utter mistake.[23]

The acceptance of Aquinas's suggestion that God is identical with His

---

[22]Ibid., pp. 86–87.
[23]Ibid., p. 47.

properties carries a high price tag. It leads to the odd suggestion that the biblical teaching that God is characterized by a variety of distinct properties is wrong. It also appears to deny the personhood of God. While the Thomist doctrine of simplicity may begin "in a pious and proper concern for God's sovereignty," Plantinga concludes, "it ends by flouting the most fundamental claims of theism."[24]

One of the most serious problems with claims made for the doctrine of simplicity is the fact that simplicity does not seem to be unique to God. There is a sense in which every human essence is also simple. Let us suppose that every human being has an essence. The essence of Socrates, for example, is the set of properties Socrates has in every possible world in which he exists. Any change in his set of essential properties would mean the end of his existence as the particular individual Socrates. Socrates' essence, then, is indivisible in the sense that none of his essential properties can be pulled out, so to speak, from his nature. His essence is an indivisible whole; it is, in other words, simple. If E (some set of properties) constitutes the essence of some being, it follows from the definition of essence that all the properties of E are necessary in the sense that the loss of any one property would alter the identity of the being in question. Since every human essence possesses properties that cannot be lost without that essence ceasing to exist, there is a sense in which every human essence is simple. It is difficult to see how simplicity is unique to God; and if it is not unique to God, simplicity is not an attribute of that being who bears the title "God."

CONCLUSION

The doctrine of simplicity was formulated to avoid the unacceptable extremes of a hyper-realism which entailed a God composed of parts and a nominalism which obliterated all differences among the divine attributes, and which, indeed, denied even that God had a nature. Plantinga's recent book makes plain that the doctrine of simplicity is also used in an attempt to avoid a dilemma that threatens the coherence of theism: if God is sovereign, then He cannot have a nature; if God has a nature, then He cannot be sovereign. Attempts to escape this dilemma by following either nominalism or Descartes lead to several grievous errors. Aquinas's attempt to escape the dilemma by equating God with His nature is unsatisfactory also because it entails conclusions that conflict with other important tenets of Christian theism.

It would appear that Christian theologians have no good reason to affirm the doctrine of divine simplicity. It seems doubtful that the doctrine adds anything significant to our understanding of God. No satisfactory analysis of simplicity has yet been given. And it is difficult to

---

[24]Ibid., pp. 53–54.

see how the property of simplicity is unique to God. Perhaps, like Emil Brunner, we should conclude that the doctrine has no practical value; it is pure speculation "which has nothing at all to do with the God of the Christian Faith."[25]

Even if my rejection of the doctrine of simplicity is correct, this does not in itself provide an escape from the dilemma noted earlier in the chapter. I have concluded that God does have a nature or set of essential properties and I have rejected Aquinas's claim that God is identical with His nature. This still leaves me with the problem of reconciling God's having a nature with His being sovereign.

This new difficulty arises for other reasons as well. Many philosophers affirm the existence of a whole host of abstract objects that supposedly exist eternally and necessarily, including properties, relations, propositions, states of affairs, and numbers. As some of my earlier chapters make clear, I have aligned myself with that tradition. Everyone in that tradition who is also a theist faces the challenge of explaining the relationship between such eternal objects and the sovereign God.

It is interesting to note that Plato, the philosopher who first drew attention to eternal objects, did not give a definitive answer as to how they are related to God. In some writings, he seemed to teach that God is subordinate to the forms.[26] But in other places, he hinted that the forms depend in some way on God.[27] During the first century A.D., the Jewish Platonist, Philo, somewhat ambiguously suggested that the eternal objects were thoughts of God. This theory appeared later in the philosophy of Plotinus and finally passed into the Christian philosophy of Augustine who spoke of the forms as *rationes aeternae*.[28] According to Augustine, eternal objects like properties and numbers "subsist" eternally in the mind of God. This is an interesting way of stating both that such entities exist eternally and that they depend upon God for their existence. If God did not exist, they would not exist.

Near the end of his book *Does God Have a Nature?* Plantinga attempts a contemporary restatement of what amounts to Augustine's position. He first states that if things like numbers, properties, relations, or propositions exist necessarily, "then God has essentially the property of affirming their existence. That property [of affirming their existence], therefore, will be part of his nature. Indeed, for any necessarily existing abstract object 0, the property of affirming the existence of 0 is part of

---

[25]Emil Brunner, *The Christian Doctrine of God* (Philadelphia: Westminster, 1950), p. 294.

[26]See Plato's *Timaeus*.

[27]See books 6 and 7 of Plato's *Republic*.

[28]Two of my books discuss this matter at greater length. See Ronald Nash, *The Word of God and the Mind of Man* (Grand Rapids: Zondervan, 1982) and Ronald Nash, *The Light of the Mind: St. Augustine's Theory of Knowledge* (Lexington: University of Kentucky Press, 1969).

God's nature. It is thus part of God's nature to say, 'Let there be the number 1; let there be 2; let there be 3 [and so on].' "[29] Plantinga is not saying that God created the numbers. That could be the case only if there was a time when the numbers began to exist. But of course the numbers have always existed. God affirms the existence of all abstract objects that exist necessarily.[30] But how does this help us understand how these abstract objects "depend" on God?

Suppose, following Plantinga, we consider these propositions:

(1) Three plus two equals five.
(2) God believes (1).
(3) "Three plus two equals five" is a necessary truth.
(4) It is part of God's nature to believe that three plus two equals five.

(1) is obviously a necessary truth. But Plantinga believes that (1) is equivalent to (2). That is, given that God is essentially omniscient, it follows that if God believes (1), then (1) is true. It is also the case that if (1) is true, then God believes (1). Plantinga's claim that (1) and (2) are equivalent is only an elaboration of the doctrine of God's essential omniscience.

But now consider the relation between (3) and (4). Is it not possible to see, Plantinga wonders, how (4) is somehow *prior* to (3)? While a full explication of its priority may be difficult, it makes sense for a theist to maintain that the necessity of "three plus two equals five" depends in some way upon it being part of God's nature to believe (3). If someone were to ask why (3) is true,[31] it would make sense to answer, "Because God believes (1)." Plantinga asks if there is a sense of the word *explain* that would make (4) the explanation of (3) while not allowing (3) to be the explanation of (4). Does it make sense to say that the truth of (4) is what *makes* (3) true? Or, to use still another expression, would it make sense to say that (4) is the ground of (3)? Plantinga admits he is asking questions that require a great deal more analysis. He does think these questions can be answered in the affirmative, and he does believe that a further exploration of these issues may help us understand how abstract objects can depend upon God without being within His control. Because their existence depends upon God, their being does not compromise the sovereignty of God.[32]

---

[29]Plantinga, *Does God Have a Nature?* p. 142.

[30]Confusion will result, however, if this is taken to mean (as in the case of propositions) that God affirms the *truth* of all propositions. Obviously, God does not. It is one thing for a proposition to exist; it is quite another for a proposition to be true. God only affirms some propositions to be true.

[31]Why, in other words, that "2 + 3 = 5" is a necessary truth.

[32]Plantinga has recently extended this line of thought in his 1982 presidential address to the Midwestern Division of the American Philosophical Association; see Alvin Plantinga, "How to Be an Anti-Realist," *Proceedings and Addresses of the American Philosophical Association* 56 (1982): 47–70.

 Immutability

Of all the current debates about the divine attributes, the disagreement over the property of immutability is the most heated. Each of the conflicting schools of thought thinks it is defending an essential element of the Christian faith. Thomists—classical theists—stress God's role as Creator. They believe that unless God is the sovereign Creator upon whom all else depends for its existence, He is not ultimate or supreme and thus does not merit our worship. The finite god of Process theology falls short of supreme ultimacy, the Thomist believes. The process theologian, on the other hand, wishes to do justice to the notion of God as one who loves, is really related to and is thus affected by the creatures who worship Him. From a process perspective, the Thomist fails to do justice to God's role as lover. As David Schindler notes,

> In what sense, if at all, can God be conceived as creator and as at once really related to, really affected by, what he creates? It would seem that both elements must be accounted for if one is finally to be faithful to the full dimensions of Christian religious experience as traditionally structured. The twin conviction that God is the ultimate creative source of whatever is of value in the universe and that he is at the same time a lover who is genuinely moved by the joys and sufferings of the universe would seem to lie at the very heart of that experience. We must therefore attempt to give a critical accounting of the experience in a way that explains, without finally explaining away, either one of its poles.[1]

The starting point for the Thomist is the conviction that if God truly is *God*, there can be no greater. God must, in other words, be perfect. But a perfect being must be incapable of change. After all, change must either be for the better or the worse. God cannot change

---

[1]David L. Schindler, "Whitehead's Challenge to Thomism on God and Creation: The Metaphysical Issues," *International Philosophical Quarterly* 19 (1979): 285.

for the better because it is impossible to improve on perfection. And obviously God cannot change for the worse since this would result in His becoming less than perfect. Therefore God cannot change. But if God cannot change, how can He enter into the kinds of interpersonal relations attributed to Him in Scripture? How can He love and care? How can the world and human beings make any difference at all to Him? How can such a God be religiously available? How, in other words, can an unchanging God enter into real relationships with His creatures? Thomism's unremitting stress on God's immutability frequently suggested a God who is a "completely impassive, indifferent metaphysical iceberg, or at least one-way unreceptive Giver, to whom my loving or not loving, my salvation or damnation, makes no difference whatever."[2] This implication has bothered a number of contemporary Neo-Thomists such as the Jesuit philosopher W. Norris Clarke.

> Now, if we are to take seriously the religious dimension of human experience . . . then it is clear that one of the central tenets of man's religious belief in God (at least in Judaeo-Christian religion) is that He is one who enters into deep personal relations of love with His creatures. And an authentic interpersonal relation of love necessarily involves not merely purely creative or one-way love, but genuine mutuality and reciprocity of love, including not only the giving of love but the joyful acceptance of it and response to it. This means that our God is a God who really cares, is really concerned with our lives and happiness, who enters into truly reciprocal personal relations with us, who responds to our prayers—to whom, in a word, our contingent world and its history somehow make a genuine difference. In short, the God of Judaeo-Christian religion must be a "religiously available" God on the personal level.[3]

Theists seem to be stuck between a rock and a hard place. If God is immutable, He cannot be the religiously available God of the Scriptures. But if God is religiously available, He cannot be the unchanging God of the philosophers. Some have tried to avoid this dilemma by saying that God is immutable in some senses and capable of change in others.

One obvious sense in which the classical theist's God must not change is in respect to His essential properties. God must be immutable in the sense that His nature and character cannot change. Nelson Pike's interesting attempt to make this point clear distinguishes between first-

---

[2] W. Norris Clarke, S.J., "A New Look at the Immutability of God," in *God, Knowable and Unknowable*, ed. Robert J. Roth, S.J. (New York: Fordham University Press, 1973), p. 45.

[3] Ibid., p. 44.

level and second-level properties of God.[4] God's first-level properties include such attributes as power, wisdom, and benevolence. What Pike calls a second-level property qualifies or modifies God's first-level properties. Pike thinks immutability is a prime example of a second-level property. "When the Christian says that God is immutable, what he means is that God cannot change as regards his power, benevolence, etc."[5] In other words, attributing immutability to God should not be taken to mean that God cannot change in *any* way. It means only that God cannot change with regard to His first-level properties; God cannot change with respect to His nature or character. God is steadfast in His character. He is unchanging in His love, power, knowledge, and holiness. Clarke asks,

> Would we want God first to be a non-loving type of person, then to grow or improve to become a loving type? Surely what we look for in Him is that He be loving, disposed to love by His very nature, that He be the eternally steadfast, faithful, indefectible Lover, unchangeable, rather than inconstant and mutable, in the fullness of His loving goodness.[6]

Thus, even if we should discover some senses in which God can change that theists can live with, God must be immutable with regard to His nature and character.

On the other hand, the immutability attributed to God should not be inconsistent with God's existence as a *person*. Clarke correctly observes that

> the immutability attributed to God must be that proper to a perfect personal being—i.e., an *immutable intention* to love and save us, which intention then includes all the adaptations and responses necessary to carry this intention through in personal dialogue with us. Thus *personal* immutability includes relational mutability.[7]

Concern for God's immutability should not exclude the possibility of God acting and interacting with His creation in an interpersonal way. The paradigm of an impersonal immutability is Aristotle's Unmoved Mover who was incapable of doing anything other than contemplating his own perfection. The change that necessarily accompanies God's interpersonal relations with His creatures is not a sign of imperfection. On the contrary, a personal God would lack perfection if He were incapable of such relations.

Change is repugnant in God only if it involves some imperfection in God's

---

[4]Nelson Pike, *God and Timelessness* (New York: Schocken Books, 1970), pp. 176ff.
[5]Ibid., p. 177.
[6]Clarke, "A New Look," p. 48.
[7]W. Norris Clarke, S.J., *The Philosophical Approach to God* (Winston-Salem, N.C.: Wake Forest University Publications, 1979), p. 108.

real being, some lack of perfection in God's inner plenitude. But if change is restricted to the relational dimension of God's consciousness, we can rethink the concept of change so that it is seen to involve no imperfection at all. The giving and receiving in a mutual relation of interpersonal love is not an imperfection *for a person*, but an integral part of the very perfection proper to a person, as we understand this theoretically so much more fully than the Greeks.[8]

Any person, including God, who could not enter into mutual relations of love would be imperfect.

Over the past ten years, the writings of W. Norris Clarke have probably been the most impressive attempt to preserve the essential elements of the traditional Christian belief in divine immutability, while taking account of the legitimate concerns expressed by process theologians. Sensitive to charges that classical Thomism tended to deny any real relationships between God and His creation, Clarke insists that the Christian God is religiously available; He is a personal and loving God. The problem that has confronted Clarke is how to preserve the loving, caring, responsive attitude associated with the biblical picture of God without undermining belief in God's perfection.

Classical theists believe process theologians have paid too high a price. In their view, the process theologian's attempt to render a coherent account of God's religious availability results in a God who is finite, impotent, and evolving; in short, a God more deserving of our pity than our worship. Is there some way to do justice to all the dimensions of the biblical picture of God? Is there a concept of God that is coherent, faithful to the biblical data, and avoids the apparent impersonalness of the Thomistic God without retreating to the impotence of the process deity? Clarke thinks there is.

Clarke believes there are latent resources within Thomistic metaphysics that can resolve the dilemma about divine immutability. Thomistic metaphysics contains a distinction between two kinds of relations: relations in the real order of a being and relations in the intentional order of a being. So long as changes occur only in God's intentional order (that is, in God's consciousness), His immutability is not compromised. Changes in God's intentional being do not require corresponding changes in God's real being. The contents of God's consciousness can be contingent, varied, and many, but this does not entail that God's intrinsic being is contingent. Though Clarke sides with the traditional Thomistic view that "God is already and from all eternity positively infinite in the fullness of His perfection," he takes a step that some interpret as a concession to Process theology. He allows that "the *expression* of [God's] love for us should be constantly growing

---

[8]Ibid., p. 95.

and developing, unfolding throughout our lives to anticipate and respond to our own contingent history of unfolding . . . love-relations with Him."[9] Clarke insists that the kind of difference the world makes to God is a difference in God's consciousness as it is intentionally related to human beings. Nothing that God creates, knows, and loves adds anything to the perfection and plenitude of His real being. God's real being is as full and complete as it can possibly be. Whatever changes may result from God's creating or knowing or loving some new creature involve new expressions and directions of His goodness and love. Clarke allows that

> in some real and genuine way God is affected positively by what we do, that He receives love from us and experiences joy *precisely because* of our responses: in a word, that His consciousness is contingently and qualitatively *different* because of what we do. All this difference remains, however, on the level of God's *relational consciousness* and therefore does not involve increase or decrease in the Infinite Plenitude of God's *intrinsic inner being* and perfection—what St. Thomas would call the "absolute" (non-relative) aspect of His perfection. God does not become a more or less perfect being because of the love we return to Him and the joy He experiences thereat (or its absence).[10]

All such changes occur only in God's consciousness (intentional order) and are not changes in God's own being. Nothing is added to make God more perfect than He was before. While the current of His love may be channeled in new directions, the current does not rise higher than its source.

Clarke is even willing to speak of novelty and enrichment in God. But, he insists, any new joy

> can only be new *determinate modalities of expression* of the already infinite intensity of actual interior joy in God, and hence can never rise higher in qualitative intensity of perfection than the already infinite Source of what all finite modalities are only limited participations. In this sense, and in this sense only, it is impossible to add to or enrich the infinite, in the sense of raising the infinite to a *qualitatively higher level of intensity* of perfection than it had before. In this sense, too, it could be said . . . that therefore there is no real "change" in God, even though such statements can be misleading by saying too little.[11]

Traditional Thomists have had at least one major problem with Clarke's type of theory, namely, that such a view implies that God's knowledge of what His creatures do is determined by or causally dependent on their actions. Clarke is sensitive to the charge that his position

---

[9]Clarke, "A New Look," p. 48.
[10]Clarke, *The Philosophical Approach to God*, p. 90.
[11]Ibid., p. 98.

implies that God's knowledge of free human acts depends in some way upon what His creatures give Him, that God learns something from us. He attempts to avoid this difficulty by reinterpreting an old Thomist theory according to which God knows the actions of His creatures by moving them. While human beings normally come to have knowledge about other persons in a passive way (by being acted upon causally), this avenue of knowledge is clearly out of the question for the classical, Thomist God. God knows about the actions of His free creatures not as a passive recipient of information He receives from them, but as an active agent whose infinite power is channeled to His creatures.

> God is constantly working in and through us with His supportive and collaborative power, supporting both the being and action of every creature. But He allows this power to be determinately channeled by the respective natures, especially the free-will decisions of creatures. Thus God knows what we are doing by how we allow His power, in itself indeterminate, to flow through us; by how we determinately channel this flow of power, according to our own free initiatives. Thus He knows not by being acted on, but through His own action in us. He knows what we are doing by *doing with us* whatever we are doing, except that it is we who supply the determinations to specify the in-itself-transcendent (and thus indeterminate) fullness of His power. To receive these determinations from creatures is not to be acted upon by them in any proper sense, though the result is determinate new knowledge in the divine consciousness. [12]

As an illustration of his thesis, Clarke asks us to imagine two men standing on opposite sides of two swinging doors. The stronger of the two men has one hand on each door and is gently pushing against them without actually forcing them. On the other side, the weaker man also applies gentle pressure to the doors while he is deciding which of the two doors he wants to open. After making his choice, he stops holding one of the doors so that the stronger man's power immediately pushes it open. Clarke thinks this example shows how the stronger man can know

> what decision the second man has freely made, not by being acted on by the latter, but by knowing where his own power is allowed to flow through. Only the negative determination or channeling of the offered power is provided by the decider. And to determine in this context is not to act upon—a point consistently overlooked it seems to me, by those who refuse to allow that God's knowledge can in any way be determined by creatures. [13]

God knows, then, not by being acted upon, but by acting.

If Clarke's reinterpretation of Thomism succeeds (and my present

---

[12]Ibid., pp. 96–97.
[13]Clarke, "A New Look," p. 69.

inclination is to think that it does), it follows that Christian theism is not forced to deny any real relations between God and His creatures; nor is it required to deny God's immutability and perfection. The Christian theist can recognize senses in which even an immutable and perfect God can change. Human beings can make a difference to God.

 Necessity

Theists have traditionally maintained that God is a necessary being. To say that God exists necessarily is to state that God *must* exist; it is to say that it is impossible for God not to exist. Whatever else may be true about God, His existence could not have happened by chance. Not only does God exist, He *must* exist, He must always have existed and He must always continue to exist.

J. N. Findlay put the theist's conviction as well as anyone (though at the time he wrote these words, he rejected the existence of a necessary being):

> We can't help feeling that the worthy object of our worship can never be a thing that merely *happens* to exist, nor one on which all other objects merely *happen* to depend. . . . And not only must the existence of *other* things be unthinkable without him, but his own non-existence must be wholly unthinkable in any circumstances. There must, in short, be no conceivable alternative to an existence properly termed "divine": God must be wholly inescapable . . . whether for thought or reality.[1]

Necessary existence is one fundamental difference between God and His creatures. Creatures exist contingently. That is, their existence might not have been; their existence is dependent on something other than themselves. God's nonexistence, on the other hand, is impossible. God's existence does not depend upon anything else; it is entirely self-caused (Latin: *a se*). A being who is less than a necessary being would be unfit to bear the title "God."

---

[1]J. N. Findlay, "Can God's Existence Be Disproved?" in *New Essays in Philosophical Theology*, ed. Antony Flew and Alasdair Macintyre (New York: Macmillan, 1955), p. 52.

TWO INTERPRETATIONS OF NECESSARY BEING

God's necessary existence has been interpreted in two quite different ways. Some have understood the notion in the sense of *logical necessity*; others have attempted to delineate a sense of *factual necessity*.

If God's necessity is understood as logical necessity, the proposition "God exists" is logically true. A logically necessary being is one that exists in every possible world. The proposition "three plus five equals eight" is necessarily true; it is true in every possible world. Likewise, if God is a logically necessary being, the proposition "God exists" is true in every possible world. To say that something is logically necessary is to claim that it is logically impossible for that thing not to exist. Just as it is logically impossible for a triangle to have four sides, so it is logically impossible for God not to exist.[2]

In recent years, many religious philosophers have given up on the notion of a logically necessary being. For reasons that will be explained shortly, they decided the concept was not only indefensible but even damaging to theism. Consequently, in order to retain a sense of necessity with respect to God, these thinkers explained God's existence as necessary in a nonlogical sense; God's existence, they said, is a factual necessity.[3]

A being who is necessary in the factual sense is one about whom three claims can be made. (1) The being is eternal, that is, it had no beginning and its existence will never end. (2) The being is self-caused, which is to say that it does not depend upon anything else for its existence. It is, in a sense already explained, *a se*. (3) Everything else that exists depends upon the necessary being for its existence. Here is the key difference between the notions of logical and factual necessity: a factually necessary being does not exist in all possible worlds. In the sense of factual necessity, the proposition "God does not exist" is not logically false. A factually necessary being is, in a sense, accidental.

THE CONTEMPORARY ATTACK ON THE NOTION OF A LOGICALLY NECESSARY BEING

A number of contemporary philosophers have all but made a career out of attacking the concept of a logically necessary God. J.J.C. Smart, for example, spoke for most of these critics when he wrote "that

---

[2]It follows then that any denial of God's existence is as self-contradictory as statements like "Some triangles have four sides." However, it is important to note in this connection that some propositions can be self-contradictory without being self-evidently so. It should be obvious that people can contradict themselves without realizing it. Therefore, the claim that "God does not exist" is self-contradictory cannot be countered by arguing that it does not *look* like a contradiction.

[3]For example, see John Hick's "God as Necessary Being," *Journal of Philosophy* 57 (1960): 725–34.

the concept of a logically necessary being is a self-contradictory concept, like the concept of a round square."[4] J. N. Findlay picked up the same theme and argued that if God is a logically necessary being, then it is impossible for God to exist. Findlay even offered a kind of ontological argument against the existence of God.[5]

Philosophical theists abandoned the notion of a logically necessary God in such numbers that it became practically impossible to find anyone willing to risk his reputation in defense of the concept. They apparently thought that the objections were so overpowering that continued advocacy of the doctrine would be detrimental to theism. Typical of the theists who abandoned the notion of a logically necessary being in favor of a nonlogical or factual necessity were John Hick, Patterson Brown, and Alvin Plantinga. (Plantinga later changed his mind and became an advocate of the doctrine of a logically necessary being.)[6]

The various arguments against the notion of a logically necessary being are reducible to two. (1) While every denial of a logically true proposition is a contradiction, denials of God's existence are not self-evident contradictions. Compare the following:

All bachelors are unmarried men.   Some bachelors are married men.
All red roses are red.   Some red roses are not red.

In each case, the contradiction is obvious. But because it is obvious, no one in possession of rational faculties goes around asserting contradictions like "Some spinsters are happily married." But all manner of people assert that God does not exist. Since it is possible to conceive the denial of "God exists," the proposition cannot be logically true. Therefore, God cannot be a logically necessary being. (2) According to the second objection, necessity should never be attributed to anything other than propositions. Since only propositions can be necessary, it is a grievous error to attribute necessity to any being, including God.

It now appears, however, that those who surrendered the doctrine of a logically necessary being acted hastily. Arguments that once seemed unanswerable are now seen to rest on premises that are under

---

[4]J. J. C. Smart, "The Existence of God," in *New Essays in Philosophical Theology*, p. 38.

[5]Findlay, "Can God's Existence Be Disproved?" However, Findlay has abandoned this particular argument. See the preface to his book, *Ascent to the Absolute* (New York: Humanities, 1970).

[6]See John Hick, "God as Necessary Being"; Patterson Brown, "St. Thomas' Doctrine of Necessary Being," *The Philosophical Review* 73 (1964): 76–90; Alvin Plantinga, "Necessary Being," in *Faith and Philosophy*, ed. Alvin Plantinga (Grand Rapids: Eerdmans, 1964). Plantinga's more recent defense of a logically necessary being can be found in his *God, Freedom and Evil* (New York: Harper and Row, 1974), pp. 85–112.

attack from a number of different directions. Consider the claim that denials of God's existence are not self-contradictory. The argument overlooks the fact that it is one thing for a proposition to be a contradiction and quite another for it to be *recognized* as one. Any number of factors might prevent some person or other from *seeing* that a given proposition is self-contradictory. Therefore, the psychological fact that a particular person does or does not recognize a proposition to be contradictory is irrelevant to whether or not that proposition is indeed contradictory.

The opponents of the concept of a logically necessary being frequently state this point in terms of conceivability. That is, they argue that a truly contradictory state of affairs should be inconceivable. Just as it is inconceivable that a triangle should have four sides, so it *should be* inconceivable that God not exist. But obviously, they argue, it is conceivable for God not to exist. People conceive of His nonexistence all the time. Therefore, God is not a logically necessary being. The weakness of this argument should have been obvious. Just because I find a state of affairs conceivable, it does not follow that it is logically possible. I might, for example, find it conceivable that the square root of 60,616 is 244. While it might be conceivable, it turns out to be logically impossible. I conclude then that the first argument against the doctrine of a logically necessary being turns out to be worthless.

The second objection is much more difficult to treat briefly because (in part) the dispute between those who contend that necessity is a feature of certain uses of language and those who insist that necessity is also a feature of reality is one of the dividing lines between rationalism and empiricism. Any clear-cut answer to the question whether there are any nonlinguistic necessities is tantamount to settling what is probably the longest-running squabble in the history of philosophy. While I suspect the disagreement can be settled (in favor of the rationalists), I have no illusions about being able to accomplish that goal within the limitations of this chapter. In fact, the issues raised by the empiricist's claim that necessity is exclusively a property of certain propositions are so demanding and complex that about all I can do is show how tenuous the empiricist's claims are and direct the reader to other writings in which the full range of issues is discussed in greater detail.

About the time when many theists retreated in full flight from a belief in a logically necessary God, philosophy in the English speaking world was still largely under the influence of one particular form of empiricism, Logical Positivism. I will take a few paragraphs to explain the positivist claim that only propositions are necessary and summarize the oft-told story of how that positivist position came to naught. Logical Positivism was a new form of empiricism that began in Vienna, Austria, and made its way to England and the United States in the 1920s and

1930s. It was popularized in *Language, Truth and Logic* by A. J. Ayer,[7] and became extremely influential after the close of World War II.

One important plank of the positivist position was something called the verification principle. Positivists thought they had discovered a criterion of meaningfulness which excluded any proposition failing the test. Only two kinds of claims can have meaning, the positivists argued: those that are true because of the meaning of their constituent terms (called analytic statements) and those that are verifiable by sense experience (called synthetic statements.) Positivists delighted in showing, or so they thought, that theological, metaphysical, and ethical statements failed to meet either criterion of meaningfulness. And so, because such statements were neither analytic (true or false by virtue of the meanings of their words) or synthetic (true or false because verifiable by experience), they were discarded as meaningless. Therefore, statements such as "God exists" were dismissed as meaningless. The positivists used their verification principle like a sledgehammer, smashing a great many of the traditional positions in philosophy. At least they did so until people began to ask about the cognitive status of the positivists' hallowed principle. What kind of statement is *it?* philosophers began to ask. As things turned out, the positivists' criterion of meaning was itself meaningless, since it could be classified as neither an analytic nor a synthetic statement. Efforts to rescue the verification principle failed.[8]

A second major plank of positivism was its claim that necessity is a property only of propositions. Actually, the positivists went further and claimed that only a particular group of propositions can be necessary, namely, those that are analytic. As it turned out, few people could agree about the exact meaning of this claim. Philosophical rationalists like Brand Blanshard had a lot of fun uncovering the ambiguities and fallacies in the positivist theory of necessary truth.[9]

But the positivist theory was not immune even from attacks by other nonpositivist empiricists. The positivist position depended on the tenability of their distinction between analytic and synthetic statements. But ironically, only a few years later, this very premise of the positivist position was being challenged by other empiricists.[10] Many theists had

---

[7]A. J. Ayer, *Language, Truth and Logic* (London: Gollancz, 1936).

[8]One could spend years reading nothing but criticisms of Logical Positivism. Two critiques of the verification principle from different perspectives are: Alvin Plantinga, *God and Other Minds* (Ithaca, N.Y.: Cornell University Press, 1967); and Brand Blanshard, *Reason and Analysis* (La Salle, Ill.: Open Court, 1962), chap. 5.

[9]Blanshard, *Reason and Analysis*, chap. 6.

[10]See W.V.O. Quine's famous article, "Two Dogmas of Empiricism," *The Philosophical Review* 60 (1951): 20–43. See also Morton White, "The Analytic and the Synthetic: An Untenable Dualism," in *John Dewey: Philosopher of Science and Freedom*, ed. Sidney Hook (New York: 1950), pp. 316–33.

abandoned the doctrine of God as a logically necessary being because they had uncritically accepted the positivist dictum that necessity could only be predicated of a particular class of propositions, namely, those that are analytic. Many philosophers today are extremely skeptical of the claim that only analytic propositions can be necessary. Others have raised new and powerful objections to those who would exclude necessity as a feature of reality.[11] Though it looked secure twenty years ago, the case against God as a logically necessary being is now seen to rest on a set of highly questionable assumptions.

While the notion of God as a logically necessary being is once again becoming respectable, new doubts are being raised about the cogency of the concept of a factually necessary being. By definition, a factually necessary being does not exist in all possible worlds. (Only a logically necessary being could exist in every possible world.) Once one recognizes, however, that there are possible worlds in which a factually necessary God does not exist, it makes sense to ask why God exists in the *real* world. But the whole point to talking about a necessary being is supposedly to defuse questions like this. The advocate of factual necessity falls into a trap of his own making. The question as to why God exists in any particular world cannot possibly arise in the case of a logically necessary God. He exists in world A or world B (and so on) because He exists in every possible world. But once a theist acknowledges that there are possible worlds in which God does not exist, the question as to why God exists in the real world gains force. Moreover, what prevents this factually necessary being from existing by chance, that is, without reason?

It appears, then, that the notion of factual necessity appeals implicitly to key features of the concept of logical necessity. Either a necessary being exists in every possible world or it does not. A logically necessary being does exist in every possible world. In this sense, it is like the number two or the concept of a square. To question *why* a necessary being exists in the real world makes no sense at all.

Those theists who sought to substitute the notion of God as a factually necessary being for that of logical necessity seem to have made two mistakes. First, they were much too hasty in surrendering the doctrine of logical necessity. Secondly, they failed to give sufficient attention to defects within the notion of a factually necessary being. They overestimated the case against the doctrine of logical necessity and underestimated the weaknesses in the notion of a factually necessary being.

---

[11]Quine has his own objections to predicating necessity of anything other than propositions. For an account of the current state of the debate as well as criticisms of Quine, see Alvin Plantinga, *The Nature of Necessity* (London: Clarendon Press, 1974).

Chapter 10

Theism Revisited

We set out to investigate two related challenges to theism.[1] According to the first of those challenges, Christian theism must be *abandoned* because its concept of God is incoherent. According to the second, the classical Christian concept of God must be *replaced* by the substitute offered by Process theology. The first challenge views God as a lost cause. The second has no problem with the existence of God, but it sees theism's concept of God as hopeless.

We have seen that the charge that the concept of God is incoherent could be raised on four different levels. Is each divine attribute internally consistent? Are conjunctions of those attributes consistent? Are the attributes consistent with other inescapable emphases of theism? And, finally, is the entire package or cluster of attributes that constitutes the theistic concept of God coherent?

I have not examined every possible challenge or completely resolved every question introduced. Many of these arguments lead into areas of philosophy that have vexed thinkers for millennia. Even if every vestige of theism were suddenly to disappear from the face of the earth, disputes between the partisans of rationalism and empiricism, between determinists and indeterminists, between realists and nominalists would continue.

The charge that the concept of a logically necessary being is incoherent rests on highly questionable assumptions. Eliminate the possible error of thinking that omnipotence entails the ability to do anything whatsoever, and no serious challenge to the coherence of this attribute remains. Medieval writers were entirely correct in insisting that divine omnipotence is limited at the very least by logical constraints. It is likely

---

[1]For convenience, we limited our discussion to Christian theism even though most of the issues investigated could have been considered in the context of Judaic or Islamic theism.

that other problems related to God's omnipotence can be settled by extending Aquinas's conviction that God's power does not apply to that which is logically impossible.

The challenge to the coherence of divine omniscience arises on a different level, namely, its compatibility with other divine attributes, like immutability, and with other important Christian concerns, like human free will. As my conclusion to chapter 4 suggested, it is not at all clear that any of the exotic theories dreamed up to reconcile divine foreknowledge and human freedom are even necessary, since the objection itself may rest on a confusion. Other challenges to God's omniscience were noted. While they sometimes raised interesting and even fascinating philosophical puzzles, none of them proved that an irreconcilable conflict exists between a belief in divine omniscience and a belief in some other essential aspect of theism.

The question of God's relation to time is much more problematic. I concluded that the doctrine of God's eternal existence is coherent even though the debate continues as to whether the attribute should be interpreted as timelessness or as unending duration. Charges about the possible incoherence of the property of simplicity are of little import, since the doctrine can be safely eliminated from the cluster of divine attributes.

The answer to the question, Is God immutable? may be yes or no depending on how the word *immutable* is understood. Certainly God is immutable in His real being. Neither His nature nor His character can change. If they did, He could no longer be God. But the demand that God enter into real relationships with His creatures requires that God experience change in the intentional order of His being. As I tried to point out, following W. Norris Clarke, recognition of this fact does not imply either that God changes in His real being or that He is acted upon by His creatures. I conclude that the concept of immutability thus interpreted is consistent with the theistic notion of God as the supreme and perfect Creator and with the concept of a God who is religiously available.

Early in chapter 2, I introduced a particular package of attributes that is frequently referred to as Thomistic theism. The elements of that package included pure actuality, immutability, impassibility, necessity, simplicity, timelessness, omnipotence, and omniscience. *This* concept of God, I believe, does have serious problems and requires modification. My own study has indicated those points where alterations could be made. Pure actuality, impassibility, and simplicity could be eliminated, and the status of timelessness is questionable. Immutability must be carefully reinterpreted as a property that applies to God's real being. Properly interpreted, the attributes of omnipotence and omniscience must continue to be regarded as essential properties of God.

What are the implications of our modification of the Thomistic concept of God for the current debate between Thomism and Process theology? Clearly, one need not choose between Thomistic theism and Process theology. We are not confronted by an exclusive disjunction that will require us to select either the entire Thomistic package of attributes or the panentheistic concept of God. There seems to be little doubt that certain features of what has been called the classical concept of God require modification. But it is quite another thing to demand that the whole classical concept be scrapped in favor of a God who is neither omnipotent nor omniscient. This is as bad a bargain as exchanging Aladdin's old lamp for a shiny new one.

But another choice before us *is* forced—the choice between theism and panentheism. Here there is no middle ground. At several points, the panentheist challenge to Thomism is warranted. But that does not require an acceptance of panentheism. I have attempted to show how modifications of the classical concept of God can be made so as to ease the objections raised against that notion by process thinkers. Once we realize the choice before us is not an either/or option, the plausibility of the process alternative fades considerably. In the decision between theism and panentheism, the choice seems clear. A being who is not essentially omnipotent or omniscient, who is not the sovereign and independent Creator, is neither worthy to receive our worship nor to bear the title "God."

Bibliography

◆

BOOKS

Bavinck, Herman. *The Doctrine of God*. Grand Rapids: Baker, 1977.

Brown, Delwin, et al. *Process Philosophy and Christian Thought*. Indianapolis: Bobbs-Merrill, 1971.

Charnock, Stephen. *The Existence and Attributes of God*. Grand Rapids: Kregel, 1958.

Clarke, Samuel. *A Demonstration of the Being and Attributes of God*. London: John and Paul Knapton, 1738.

Clarke, W. Norris, S.J. *The Philosophical Approach to God*. (Winston-Salem, N.C.: Wake Forest University Press, 1979.

Cobb, John B., Jr., *A Christian Natural Theology*. Philadelphia: Westminster, 1966.

Cobb, John B., Jr., and Griffin, David Ray. *Process Theology: An Introductory Exposition*. Philadelphia: Westminster, 1976.

Cousins, Ewert, ed. *Process Theology*. New York: Newman Press, 1971.

Garrigou-Lagrange, R., O.P. *God: His Existence and His Nature*. 2 vols. St. Louis: B. Herder, 1936.

Geach, Peter. *Providence and Evil*. New York: Cambridge University Press, 1977.

Hartshorne, Charles. *The Divine Relativity*. New Haven: Yale University Press, 1948.

Hartshorne, Charles, and Reese, William L., eds. *Philosophers Speak of God*. Chicago: University of Chicago Press, 1953.

Kenny, Anthony. *The God of the Philosophers*. Oxford: Clarendon Press, 1979.

Mascall, E. L. *He Who Is*. London: Longmans, Green and Co., 1962.

———. *The Openness of Being*. Philadelphia: Westminster, 1971.

Neville, Robert C. *Creativity and God*. New York: Seabury, 1980.

Ogden, Schubert. *The Reality of God and Other Essays*. New York: Harper and Row, 1966.

117

Penelhum, Terence. *Religion and Rationality*. New York: Random House, 1971.

Pike, Nelson. *God and Timelessness*. New York: Schocken, 1970.

Pittenger, Norman. *Catholic Faith in a Process Perspective*. Maryknoll, N.Y.: Orbis, 1981.

———. *Process Thought and Christian Faith*. New York: Macmillan, 1968.

Plantinga, Alvin. *Does God Have a Nature?* Milwaukee: Marquette University Press, 1980.

———. *God, Freedom and Evil*. New York: Harper and Row, 1974.

Ross, James. *Philosophical Theology*. Indianapolis: Bobbs-Merrill, 1969.

Stever, Axel D., and McLendon, James William, Jr. *Is God GOD?* Nashville: Abingdon, 1981.

Swinburne, Richard. *The Coherence of Theism*. Oxford: Clarendon, 1977.

Urban, Linwood, and Walton, Douglas N., eds. *The Power of God*. New York: Oxford University Press, 1978.

Ward, Keith. *Rational Theology and the Creativity of God*. New York: Pilgrim, 1982.

Whitehead, Alfred North. *Process and Reality*. New York: Harper and Row, 1960 reprint.

ARTICLES

Adams, Marilyn McCord. "Is the Existence of God a 'Hard' Fact?" *Philosophical Review* 76 (1967): 492–503.

Adams, Robert Merrihew. "Middle Knowledge and the Problem of Evil." *American Philosophical Quarterly* 14 (1977): 109–17.

Ahern, Dennis M. "Foreknowledge: Nelson Pike and Newcomb's Problem." *Religious Studies* 15 (1979): 475–90.

Baumer, Michael. "The Role of 'Inevitability of Time T' in Aquinas' Solution to the Problem of Future Contingents." *The New Scholasticism* 53 (1979): 147–67.

Blumenfeld, David. "On the Compossibility of the Divine Attributes." *Philosophical Studies* 34 (1978): 91–103.

Brown, Patterson. "Religious Morality." *Mind* 72 (1963): 235–44.

Burrell, David B., C.S.C. "Does Process Theology Rest on a Mistake?" *Theological Studies* 43 (1982): 125–35.

Cargile, James. "On Omnipotence." *Nous* 1 (1967): 201–5.

Casteñada, Hector-Neri. "Omniscience and Indexical Reference." *Journal of Philosophy* 64 (1967): 203–10.

Clarke, W. Norris, S.J. "A New Look at the Immutability of God." In *God, Knowable and Unknowable*, edited by Robert J. Roth, 43–72. New York: Fordham University Press, 1973.

Cowan, J. L. "The Paradox of Omnipotence Revisited." *Canadian Journal of Philosophy* 3 (1974): 435–45.

Daher, Adel. "God and Factual Necessity." *Religious Studies* 6 (1970): 23–39.

Demarest, Bruce A. "Process Theology and the Pauline Doctrine of the Incarnation." In *Pauline Studies*, edited by Donald A. Hagner and Murray J. Harris, 122–42. Grand Rapids: Eerdmans, 1980.

_____. "Process Trinitarianism." In *Perspectives on Evangelical Theology*, edited by Kenneth S. Kantzer and Stanley N. Gundry, 15–36. Grand Rapids: Baker, 1979.

Donceel, Joseph, S.J. "God in Transcendental Thomism." *Logos* 1 (1980): 53–63.

Dummett, Michael. "On Bringing About the Past." *Philosophical Review* 73 (1964): 338–59.

Edwards, Rem B. "The Pagan Dogma of the Absolute Unchangeableness of God." *Religious Studies* 14 (1978): 305–13.

Engelbretson, George. "The Incompatibility of God's Existence and Omnipotence." *Sophia* 10 (1971): 28–31.

Eslick, Leonard. "The Meanings of Power." *The New Scholasticism* 48 (1968): 289–92.

Ford, Lewis. "The Immutable God and Father Clarke." *The New Scholasticism* 49 (1975): 189–99.

_____. "The Search for the Source of Creativity." *Logos* 1 (1980): 45–52.

_____. "The Viability of Whitehead's God for Christian Theology." *Proceedings of the American Catholic Philosophical Association* 44 (1970): 141–51.

Frankfurt, Harry. "The Logic of Omnipotence." *Philosophical Review* 73 (1964): 262–63.

Gillman, Jerome. "Omnipotence and Impeccability." *The New Scholasticism* 51 (1977): 21–37.

_____. "The Paradox of Omnipotence and Perfection." *Sophia* 14 (1975): 31–39.

Helm, Paul. "Divine Foreknowledge and Facts." *Canadian Journal of Philosophy* 4 (1974): 305–15.

_____. "Foreknowledge and Possibility." *Canadian Journal of Philosophy* 6 (1976): 731–34.

_____. "God and Spacelessness." *Philosophy* 55 (1980): 211–21.

_____. "God and Whatever Comes to Pass." *Religious Studies* 14 (1978): 315–23.

_____. "Omnipotence and Change." *Philosophy* 51 (1976): 454–61.

_____. "Timelessness and Foreknowledge." *Mind* 84 (1975): 515–27.

Hick, John. "God as Necessary Being." *Journal of Philosophy* 57 (1960): 725–34.

Hill, William. "In What Sense Is God Infinite? A Thomistic Perspective." *The Thomist* 42 (1978): 14–27.

_____. "Two Gods of Love: Aquinas and Whitehead." *Listening* 14 (1976): 249–64.

Hoffman, Joshua. "Pike on Possible Worlds, Divine Foreknowledge, and Human Freedom." *Philosophical Review* 88 (1979): 433–42.

Holt, Dennis C. "Foreknowledge and the Necessity of the Past." *Canadian Journal of Philosophy* 6 (1976): 721–30.

_____. "Timelessness and the Metaphysics of Temporal Existence." *American Philosophical Quarterly* 18 (1981): 149–56.

Hoitenga, Dewey J., Jr. "Logic and the Problem of Evil." *American Philosophical Quarterly* 4 (1967): 114–26.

Hopkins, Jasper. "Augustine on Foreknowledge and Free Will." *International Journal for Philosophy of Religion* 8 (1977): 111–26.

Hudson, W. Donald. "The Concept of Divine Transcendence." *Religious Studies* 15 (1979): 197–210.

Kelly, Anthony J. "God: How Near a Relation?" *The Thomist* 34 (1970): 191–229.

Kenny, Anthony. "Divine Foreknowledge and Human Freedom." In *Aquinas: A Collection of Critical Essays*, edited by Anthony Kenny, 255–70. New York: Doubleday, 1969.

———. "God and Necessity." In *British Analytical Philosophy*, edited by Bernard Williams and Alan Montefiore, 131–51. New York: Humanities Press, 1966.

———. "Necessary Being." *Sophia* 1 (1962): 1–8.

Khamara, E. J. "In Defense of Omnipotence." *Philosophical Quarterly* 28 (1978): 215–28.

Kretzmann, Norman. "Omniscience and Immutability." *Journal of Philosophy* 63 (1966): 409–21.

La Croix, Richard. "Augustine on the Simplicity of God." *The New Scholasticism* 51 (1977): 453–69.

———. "Wainwright, Augustine and God's Simplicity." *The New Scholasticism* 53 (1979): 124–27.

Londey, David. "God and the Stone Paradox: Three Comments." *Sophia* 10 (1971): 23–25.

Luhman, Reginald S. "The Concept of God: Some Philosophical Considerations." *The Evangelical Quarterly* 54 (1982): 88–104.

Mackie, J. W. "Omnipotence." *Sophia* 1 (1962): 13–25.

Mann, William E. "Divine Simplicity." *Religious Studies* 19 (1983).

Mason, David R. "Can God Be Both Perfect and Free?" *Religious Studies* 18 (1982): 191–200.

Mavrodes, George. "Defining Omnipotence." *Philosophical Studies* 32 (1977): 191–202.

———. "Some Puzzles Concerning Omnipotence." *Philosophical Review* 72 (1963): 221–23.

O'Briant, Walter H. "Determinism, Fatalism and Theism." *Sophia* 10 (1971): 22–26.

Pegis, Anton. "Molina and Human Liberty." In *Jesuit Thinkers of the Renaissance*, edited by Gerard Smith, S.J., 75–131. Milwaukee: Marquette University Press, 1939.

Pike, Nelson. "Divine Foreknowledge, Human Freedom and Possible Worlds." *Philosophical Review* 86 (1977): 209–16.

———. "Divine Omniscience and Voluntary Action." *Philosophical Review* 74 (1965): 27–46.

_____. "Of God and Freedom: A Rejoinder." *Philosophical Review* 75 (1966): 369–79.

_____. "Omnipotence and God's Ability to Sin." *American Philosophical Quarterly* 6 (1969): 208–16.

Peterson, Michael L. "Orthodox Christianity, Wesleyanism, and Process Theology." *Wesleyan Theological Journal* 15 (1980): 45–58.

Plantinga, Alvin. "Necessary Being." In *Faith and Philosophy*, edited by Alvin Plantinga, 97–108. Grand Rapids: Eerdmans, 1964.

Prior, Arthur. "The Formalities of Omniscience." In *Readings in the Philosophy of Religion*, edited by Baruch Brody, 413–27. Englewood Cliffs, N.J.: Prentice-Hall, 1974.

Puccetti, Roland. "Before Creation." *Sophia* 3 (1964): 24–26.

Quinn, Philip. "Divine Foreknowledge and Divine Freedom." *International Journal for Philosophy of Religion* 9 (1978): 219–40.

Rosenkrantz, Gary, and Hoffman, Joshua. "What an Omnipotent Agent Can Do." *International Journal for Philosophy of Religion* 11 (1980): 1–19.

Rowe, William. "Augustine on Foreknowledge and Free Will." *Review of Metaphysics* 18 (1964): 356–63.

Saunders, John Turk. "Of God and Freedom." *Philosophical Review* 75 (1966): 219–25.

Savage, C. Wade. "The Paradox of the Stone." *Philosophical Review* 76 (1967): 74–79.

Schindler, David L. "Creativity as Ultimate: Reflections on Actuality in Whitehead, Aristotle, and Aquinas." *International Philosophical Quarterly* 13 (1973): 161–71.

_____. "Whitehead's Challenge to Thomism on God and Creation: The Metaphysical Issues." *International Philosophical Quarterly* 19 (1979): 285–99.

Schrader, David E. "A Solution to the Stone Paradox." *Synthese* 42 (1979): 255–64.

Stump, Eleonore. "Petitionary Prayer." *American Philosophical Quarterly* 16 (1979): 81–91.

Stump, Eleonore, and Kretzmann, Norman. "Eternity." *Journal of Philosophy* 78 (1981): 429–58.

Sturch, R. L. "The Problem of the Divine Eternity." *Religious Studies* 10 (1974): 487–93.

Sutherland, Stewart R. "God, Time and Eternity." *Proceedings of the Aristotelian Society* 79 (1978–1979): 103–21.

Swinburne, Richard. "Omnipotence." *American Philosophical Quarterly* 10 (1973): 231–37.

Teske, Roland J., S.J. "Omniscience, Omnipotence and Divine Transcendence." *The New Scholasticism* 53 (1979): 277–94.

_____. "Properties of God and the Predicaments in *De Trinitate* V." *The Modern Schoolman* 59 (1981): 1–19.

Tomkinson, J. L. "Divine Sempiternity and Atemporality." *Religious Studies* 18 (1982): 177–89.

Wainwright, William J. "Augustine on God's Simplicity: A Reply." *The New Scholasticism* 53 (1979): 118–23.

Westphal, Merold. "Temporality and Finitude in Hartshorne's Theism." *Review of Metaphysics* 19 (1966): 550–64.

Whitney, Barry L. "Divine Immutability in Process Philosophy and Contemporary Thomism." *Horizons* 7 (1980): 49–68.

Wolterstorff, Nicholas. "God Everlasting." In *God and the Good*, edited by Clifton Orlebeke and Lewis Smedes, 181–203. Grand Rapids: Eerdmans, 1975.

Index of Names

◆

Index of Subjects

◆